Japan's Far More Female Future

Japan's Far More Female Future

Increasing Gender Equality and Reducing Workplace Insecurity Will Make Japan Stronger

Bill Emmott

OXFORD
UNIVERSITY PRESS

OXFORD
UNIVERSITY PRESS

Great Clarendon Street, Oxford, OX2 6DP,
United Kingdom

Oxford University Press is a department of the University of Oxford.
It furthers the University's objective of excellence in research, scholarship,
and education by publishing worldwide. Oxford is a registered trade mark of
Oxford University Press in the UK and in certain other countries

© Bill Emmott 2020

The moral rights of the author have been asserted

First Edition published in 2020

Impression: 1

Published in the United States of America by Oxford University Press
198 Madison Avenue, New York, NY 10016, United States of America

British Library Cataloguing in Publication Data
Data available

Library of Congress Control Number: 2020937782

ISBN 978–0–19–886555–1

Printed and bound in Great Britain by
Clays Ltd, Elcograf S.p.A.

Links to third party websites are provided by Oxford in good faith and
for information only. Oxford disclaims any responsibility for the materials
contained in any third party website referenced in this work.

Preface

When Japan hosted its first Olympic Games, in 1964, the opening ceremony encompassed an important but subtle piece of symbolism. The Olympic flame was carried up its last 160 steps by a 19-year-old student called Sakai Yoshinori[1] who had been born, near Hiroshima, on the very day the atomic bomb was dropped, 6 August 1945. 'Atomic Boy', as he became known, bore twin messages: that Japan had been a victim of an unbelievable horror; and that the once-defeated nation had now been reborn as a modern, democratic state.

For Japan's second Olympic Games, originally scheduled for fifty-six years later in 2020, that sort of political symbolism was no longer needed. No one but a few Chinese or North Korean propagandists can any longer doubt that modern Japan is a peaceful, law-abiding democracy. The fact that the global Covid-19 pandemic sadly forced the Games to be postponed by a year means that we will have to wait longer to know who has acted as Sakai-san's[2] successor as the final torchbearer in the opening ceremony. Yet it will still be a highly symbolic choice. In what it called its 'Basic Policy'[3] for the opening ceremony, the Tokyo 2020 Organising Committee stated the following: 'When people look back on the Tokyo 2020 Games in 50 or 100 years' time, the Games should be seen to have been a catalyst for change in culture, society and values leading to the realisation of a more sustainable, spiritually richer, happier society.'

To represent Japanese society today, one potential choice could have been that of a centenarian, even if in that case it might be necessary to replace the steps up to the Olympic urn with an

---

[1] Christopher Harding, *Japan Story: In Search of a Nation 1850 to the Present* (Allen Lane, 2018), 257.

[2] Sakai Yoshinori himself died in 2014 at the age of 69 having spent his career as a journalist at Fuji Television.

[3] https://tokyo2020.org/en/games/ceremony/concept/.

escalator. A centenarian would have been apt even for this celebration of youth and vigour because such a person would have represented the vast demographic change that has taken place in Japan since 1964, which has turned it from what was then a young country into what is today the world's oldest society, one featuring more than 70,000 people of over 100 years of age. Take the artist Shinoda Toko, who features in Chapter 7 and celebrated her 107th birthday in March 2020. Like anyone of that age, she bridges the half century between the two Tokyo Games: she was even commissioned to produce an artwork for one of the rooms of the National Stadium that was used in the 1964 Games and she is still producing art to this day.

Yet to be 'a catalyst for change in culture, society and values' is a somewhat different aspiration from simply representing today's Japan. The enthusiastic and positive reception given to the national team for the 2019 Rugby World Cup, with its mixture of native Japanese and immigrant players and its mixed-race captain, Michael Leitch,[4] led to much speculation that the 2020 'catalyst' Olympic torchbearer might again be a mixed-race Japanese sportsperson, with attention focusing on Osaka Naomi, the part-Japanese, part-Haitian tennis star. Rather than racial background, however, the most relevant symbol of change would be gender: Japan is not becoming markedly more multi-racial but the role of women is indeed on the rise and could benefit greatly from symbolic catalysis. We already know that a gesture in this direction has been made by commissioning a female director, Kawase Naomi, who also features in Chapter 7, to produce the official film for the 2020 Olympic Games. The official film[5] of the 1964 Games, *Tokyo Olympiad*, considered something of an epic, was directed by Ichikawa Kon.

Admittedly, two of the cities that played a leading role as venues for the Rugby World Cup and will eventually do so again for the Olympics, Tokyo and Yokohama, are already presided over by women: Koike Yuriko, the Governor of Tokyo, and Hayashi Fumiko, the Mayor of Yokohama (both featured in Chapter 6). They however

---

[4] Michael Leitch was born in New Zealand to a Fijian mother and European New Zealander father, and moved to Japan as a teenager, taking Japanese citizenship in 2013.

[5] https://www.olympic.org/news/relive-kon-ichikawa-s-iconic-film-about-the-1964-games.

are exceptions in a political world still heavily dominated by men. But society as a whole is changing, with the number of women taking up prominent positions rising steadily, if from a low base, and with new generations of young women emerging who have at last benefited from university educations in almost equal numbers to their male contemporaries. Those new generations are setting off to forge lives that are likely to be completely different to those of their mothers or grandmothers and will have a much more apparent impact on their country and all its many activities and characteristics than their forebears were able to have. Japan's future will be far more female than its past, so it would be highly pertinent to reflect that future in the choice of final torchbearer, which would also be a forward-looking sign of confidence and optimism about the country's recovery from the severe economic effects of the pandemic.

That future truly will be very different from the past. Throughout my nearly forty years of writing about Japan, it has been normal and often fruitful for outsiders to look at the country as a pioneer, a place from which lessons can be learned for the rest of the world. During the 1960s this was true of the country's rapid economic development and modernization, during the 1970s of the country's environmental clean-up and rapid adjustment to greater energy efficiency, during the 1980s of the country's excellent use of (male) human capital to develop, implement, and exploit the new technologies of the time, while during the 1990s the principal lessons came to be of how to maintain social cohesion even while making a thorough and unfortunate mess of dealing with what at that date had been the worst financial crash experienced by an advanced economy since 1929. Even so, twenty years later when Europeans and Americans were grappling with their own financial disaster, they again looked to Japan for lessons on how to prevent a drama from turning into a catastrophe. One aspect of social and economic development in which Japan has never been a pioneer, however, has been that of gender equality, for it has consistently been a laggard in terms of providing freer choices and more equal rights and opportunities to the female half of the population. And it remains a laggard today.

This matters greatly. One of the most frequent questions posed to someone who, like me, offers themselves as a political economist studying Japan, concerns what the future will hold for such an ageing society, with its population dropping by half a million each year. Given the title of one of my previous books,[6] the question is often posed in the following form: 'Will the sun rise again for Japan in the 2020s, or will it set?' The truth of course is that we cannot know the future, even though economists have arguably created a rod for their own backs by inventing the practice of economic forecasting. Looking at Japan today, however, that question about the future can best be responded to by posing a question in return: If you were to be able to tell me whether or how rapidly women will achieve in Japan the sort of role in terms of work and of political, intellectual, and organizational leadership that they have already achieved in most West European and North American countries, then I would have a better idea of Japan's overall future and of the brightness and warmth of that symbolic or metaphorical sun.

The reason why women's role in Japanese society now looks so central is that the country faces two key determinants of its economic and social future. One concerns how productive is its use of human capital, the very thing that Japan seemed so excellent at during the 1980s when the humans who had deployable capital as they emerged from schools and universities were primarily male. As Chapter 1 will argue, the country is in a paradoxical situation in which its people are now better educated than ever before, especially women, and yet large numbers work in unproductive ways, with less training than their forebears received and stuck in lowly paid, drudge occupations. The reward for escaping that paradox and returning to an excellent and fulfilling use of human capital would be immense both in economic and social terms. The largest component of such an escape would involve women, for they are the most poorly used resource, but it would also involve men, many of whom are also currently trapped in drudge occupations.

The second key determinant of Japan's economic and social future is fertility, or rather marriage and the formation of families. Anyone who knows Japan will know that this is a country in which children are adored and is probably the safest in the world in which

---

[6] *The Sun Also Sets: The Limits to Japan's Economic Power* (Simon & Schuster, 1989).

to raise them, one where groups of young children can be seen travelling together on buses or trains without supervision, clad in their smart uniforms and wearing ubiquitous brightly coloured backpacks. They will also know that marriage has also long been a prized institution, one whose elaborate ceremonials have formed the basis of the business models of luxury hotels in every town and city across the nation, as well as for Shinto shrines. So it is particularly concerning that not only has the country's fertility rate fallen further than those of many other advanced countries but so also has its marriage rate. A main reason for this has been the spread of financial insecurity during the past three decades, preventing low-skilled men in particular from performing their traditional function as breadwinners.

That is why, for the new Japan being represented by these sporting spectacles of 2019 and 2021, the role of women has become so important. As in other countries, gender equality in Japan can feel an uncomfortable issue, whether it involves working practices, family roles, sexual harassment and violence, discrimination, management styles, or all sorts of other aspects. To move towards greater equality represents a big change for a country that has for so long operated with quite markedly gendered roles although this is, if we are honest, a change that all countries have been experiencing at differing speeds and times, and frequently struggling with. It can involve laws and public policy but it mainly involves what we tend with great vagueness to call culture: the way in which people interact with one another, the institutions they build and adapt and within which those interactions take place, and the presumptions and attitudes they bring to those interactions.

Reflecting that mixture, the book is divided into three parts: the first, an analysis of the data, laws, public policy, and institutions surrounding Japan's socio-economic development and women's roles in it; the second, field research consisting of interviews with twenty-one women who can be considered success stories in their particular fields, organized according to themes; and finally the third, of conclusions and recommendations.

Acknowledgements

The starting point for this book was a chance encounter with two Japanese women on a boat crossing a fjord in Norway, where my wife and I were on holiday. Chatting to them during the journey our fellow tourists proved to be a daughter and her mother, and the daughter, Hirata Michiko, turned out to own an art gallery in Nihombashi in central Tokyo. Asked what kind of artists she represented, she answered that one of her best clients was a 103-year-old female abstract artist called Shinoda Toko, who happened also to have just published a book which had sold more than half a million copies. This sounded quite a remarkable woman, who I immediately thought would be interesting to meet. My wife went a step further: 'You've never really talked to Japanese women, have you,' she said. 'Why don't you do your next book about Japanese women?'

It was a fine idea. Chief among those who helped me turn that idea into this book was Onoki Kyoko, a researcher whom I have known since we both worked for different foreign publications in the 1980s in a part of the old Nikkei building in Otemachi that was known as 'gaijin corner'. Onoki-san helped me to find and interview the twenty-one 'success stories' in Part Two, provided invaluable research, helped with Japanese interpretation and translation, and eventually checked all sorts of facts.

Female experts were an important source of information and understanding, for it is obvious that men might not necessarily be reliable or particularly conscientious observers on gender inequality in Japan. Particular thanks must go to Bando Mariko, president of Showa Women's University and a great proponent of female empowerment; to my good friend Osawa Machiko, director of the Research Center for Women and Careers at Japan Women's University; to Fujiwara Mariko, former director of the Hakuhodo Institute for Life and Living, who had been one of the few professional women whom I had found to talk to when I was a foreign correspondent in Japan in the 1980s; to journalist friends such as Doden Aiko of NHK and Iizuka Keiko of Yomiuri Shimbun, off whom I bounced many ideas; to Sugeno Saori, of Daiwa Institute of Research, who hosted a very informative lunch with some female professional contacts; and to my longtime friend Yamashita Yuko, professor of marketing at Hitotsubashi University and convenor of that college's 'Hermes' network of female alumni, who organized a roundtable to discuss the alumni survey cited in Chapter 2. Moreover, as the opening anecdote indicated, I must give special thanks to Hirata Michiko for both inspiring me to meet Shinoda Toko and for arranging it. And of course I give especially warm thanks to all the twenty-one women in Part Two who gave up their time to tell me their stories and share their ideas, and everyone else I spoke to for the book.

At the end of the process, to check that my thoughts were not going crazy, I met up with two quite famous female specialists on this issue who both provided crucial guidance: Kathy Matsui of Goldman Sachs, who is generally credited with popularizing the term 'womenomics' in her now five studies on the case for greater gender equality in Japan; and the doyenne among female independent board directors, Fukushima Tachibana Sakie, who has been deeply involved in addressing gender diversity issues at the Keidanren and Keizai Doyukai.

A crucial part of the research for the book was done during a visiting fellowship at All Souls College, Oxford, in the 2017–18 academic year: I thank the warden, John Vickers, and the fellows and staff for making my time at All Souls so fruitful and stimulating. Also in Oxford, the Nissan Institute for Japanese Studies at St Antony's College kindly invited me to give a seminar in October 2018 at which I was able to try out some of the thinking and research in this book, as also did the University of Tokyo in May 2019 when they kindly made me an Ushioda Fellow of their new research institute, Tokyo College, and invited me to give a public lecture on *Japan's Far More Female Future*.

For getting the book to publication I thank my long-time Japanese agent, Tamaoki Manami and her colleagues at the Tuttle-Mori Agency in Tokyo, and my friend Felicity Bryan in Oxford who introduced me to OUP and to Adam Swallow, the commissioning editor who took this project on and saw it efficiently and carefully to its conclusion. Kawakami Junko, who acted as translator for the Japanese version of this text, also pointed out some errors and infelicities, as well as providing much helpful encouragement. Two former colleagues from my time at *The Economist*, Christopher Wilson and Adam Meara, provided the data and drew the fourteen figures.

As always, full responsibility for any remaining omissions, errors, or infelicities in this book and in the thinking that surrounds it rests entirely with the author.

Contents

List of Figures

Note on Japanese Names

Japanese names appear in this book in the standard Japanese order of family name followed by given name: Abe Shinzo rather than Shinzo Abe. Roughly from the 1870s onwards, as Japan opened up to contact with Europeans and Americans after two centuries of almost complete exclusion, most Japanese politicians, government officials, business leaders, and academics opted for a divided practice: they used the Japanese name order at home but reversed their names into the western order when abroad or dealing with international matters. Effective from 1 January 2020, however, the government adopted an official practice of using the Japanese name order at all times, at home or abroad. People not in the government will no doubt continue to follow a mixed practice in future but for clarity's sake this book has followed the official rule for all Japanese names. On second mention, Japanese are referred to with the honorific -san (e.g. Abe-san). All other names, including those of Japanese Americans (e.g. Kathy Matsui), are given in the western order and on second mention given titles such as Mr or Ms.

PART ONE

HUMAN CAPITAL AND THE SOURCES OF JAPAN'S VULNERABILITY

1
The Legacy of the *Heisei* Era, 1989–2019

The year 1989 proved to be momentous, all around the world. In China, anger at inflation and economic instability in many cities nationwide mutated into pro-democracy protests in Beijing which were brought to a close on 4 June when troops killed unknown numbers of demonstrators in the streets around Tiananmen Square and a military crackdown then ensued throughout the country. There, a potential turning point between forms of government was averted, while in Europe such points were spinning all over the continent. On the same day, the Solidarity movement won an overwhelming victory in Poland's first free elections, which set the country on its path towards independence from the Soviet Union and laid the way for mostly peaceful revolutions elsewhere in the Soviet bloc and the demise of the Soviet Union itself a year and a half later. In November, the Berlin Wall was breached and the border between West and East Germany was opened, setting that country on its path towards reunification the following year. For once, it was not mere hyperbole to say that history had been made, both for good and for ill.

History was also made in Japan in 1989, though in rather different and more morally neutral ways. The year began with the death of Emperor Hirohito on 7 January, after sixty-two years on the Chrysanthemum Throne. This meant that history had a new beginning in an official sense, since the *Showa* imperial period (and therefore calendar) thus came to an end, to be succeeded the following day by a new period as Hirohito's eldest son, Akihito, became emperor and the era name of *Heisei*, or 'peace everywhere', was announced. Yet 1989 also proved to mark a turning point in an unofficial sense, for it proved to be the last year of what at the time had been thought of as a golden age of economic growth and prosperity but which subsequently became known as the 'bubble era' (*baburu jidai*) or 'bubble economy'. That transformation from an apparent golden age to one of financial, economic, and social stress ended up shattering domestic and international perceptions alike about what made the country tick, about the institutions, culture, and structures that had seemed to characterize Japan. It broke cherished assumptions about what worked and what did not but also helped set those institutions and features on a new course. Until it was surpassed by the 2008 financial collapse that occurred in the United States and much of Western Europe, Japan's financial crash of 1990–2 counted as the most severe such event in any developed country since 1929.

The bursting of the bubble was also something rather uncharacteristic for modern Japan: a sudden, dramatic, newsworthy event. For, perhaps as a reaction to its tumultuous first half of the twentieth century, Japan has developed a political and corporate culture that seems deliberately to try to avoid dramas and big occasions. This trait can make the country a challenging place for foreign correspondents as well as for historians seeking catchy labels. But it also means that the real art for journalists and academics alike is not chiefly one of interpreting events but rather that of detecting and analysing the changes that take place more gradually, below the surface, out of sight of the TV cameras. Which makes it convenient for the present purpose that the calendar encompassing the past three decades has now come to an official end with the abdication in May 2019 of Emperor Akihito and the succession of his son Naruhito. The *Heisei* period is thus over, with Naruhito's reign officially known as *Reiwa*, or 'beautiful harmony'. This gives us a marker and a more than adequate time-frame within which to detect and analyse change, whether in politics, the economy, or society.

If you were just to look at the political headlines, you could be forgiven for thinking that not much had actually changed during the *Heisei* period, apart from the fact that China has replaced Japan as the world's economic-growth champion and the West's commercial and political bogeyman. After all, the Liberal Democratic Party remains firmly in power today, just as it was throughout the period 1955–89, having been out of government just for three of the *Heisei* years (2009–12) although it was also weakened and needed to govern through coalitions at other times. The US–Japan Security Treaty remains the anchor of Japanese foreign, defence, and security policy just as it has been ever since it was first signed in 1951, with the vaunted 'Ron–Yasu' golfing and diplomatic relationship of the 1980s between President Ronald Reagan and Prime Minister Nakasone Yasuhiro now being replaced by a 'Don–Shinzo' relationship, though fewer use that abbreviation for the slavish attention paid by Prime Minister Abe Shinzo to President Donald Trump since his election in November 2016. The fall of the Soviet Union has turned Russia from being an ever-present threat to a potential negotiating partner over the group of four previously Japanese-held islands at the southern end of the Kurile chain that the USSR took control of in 1945, but no settlement has been reached. China and North Korea remain Japan's leading security threats. Enmity and resentment over the history of Japanese occupation and war bedevilled the relationship between Japan and South Korea in 1989 and it still did in 2019—arguably even more so.

Foreign and security policies are such creatures of history and geography that they cannot really be expected to change markedly even over three decades, unless and until the geopolitics of great-power relations alters at a global level to force countries and regions to reposition themselves. But society and the economy are a different matter. The *Heisei* decades have left those quite radically altered, in ways that have in turn altered some of the country's main institutions, both formal and informal. Those alterations and evolutions form the essential background and starting point for this book, as the way in which Japan's society and economy changed during the *Heisei* period carries implications for how the country is likely to evolve during the next several decades too. The purpose of this book is to gauge what factors are likely to shape those coming decades, particularly the question of gender equality and women's role in society, the economy, and politics, an issue on which Japan differs especially markedly from other advanced countries.

The 1980s, which proved to be the final decade of the *Showa* era, had been launched, in a sense, by an American book[1] with a beguilingly flattering title—*Japan as Number One* by Ezra Vogel, a sociology professor from Harvard University—which not surprisingly became a bestseller in Japanese translation. My own engagement with Japan began in 1983 when *The Economist* decided to post me there as their Tokyo correspondent. Professor Vogel's book topped my advance reading list, of course, but work by another American academic, Chalmers Johnson,[2] introduced me to the assumption that Japanese bureaucrats, led by the powerful Ministry for International Trade and Industry (MITI), had played a central role in guiding industrial development and innovation, notably including the successful adjustment the country had made to the twin 'shocks' of the early 1970s from sharply rising oil prices and the forced revaluation of the yen. The writings of a British scholar, Ronald Dore,[3] taught me how peaceful and collaborative industrial relations had emerged in Japan since the strike-ridden 1950s and early 1960s and had enabled manufacturing companies to develop efficient and innovative methods of management and factory organization, later to become famous as 'just-in-time' supply chains and *kaizen* or continuous improvement systems. Two American business consultants, James Abegglen and George Stalk, supplemented this political economy reading list during my posting in Tokyo with their seminal 1985 study of how Japanese companies turned those methods into world-beating success, *Kaisha*[4] (Japanese for company).

It didn't take long for a new resident to notice that Japan was then a highly patriarchal society, in which marriages were often arranged and divorces were rare because jobs for women were scarce and poorly paid, making life as a divorcee financially unviable. It was also a society in which a superb primary and secondary school

---

[1] Ezra F. Vogel, *Japan as Number One: Lessons for America* (Harvard University Press, 1979).

[2] Chalmers A. Johnson, *MITI and the Japanese Miracle: The Growth of Industrial Policy, 1925–75* (Stanford University Press, 1982).

[3] Ronald Dore, *British Factory, Japanese Factory* (Allen & Unwin, 1973).

[4] James C. Abegglen and George Stalk Jr, *Kaisha: How Marketing, Money and Manpower Strategy, Not Management Style, Make the Japanese World-Beaters* (Basic Books, 1985).

system gave men high levels of numeracy and literacy which equipped them for secure, 'lifetime' employment during which companies would train them in the specific skills they needed. The stereotypical woman, 'Mrs Watanabe' as financial analysts liked to name her, handled the household budget and any securities investments the family might be able to afford. She might have studied after leaving high school at a two-year Junior College, on a curriculum commonly featuring home economics, but was very unlikely to have been accepted by a proper, four-year university course, in the even unlikelier event that her parents had allowed her to apply, and if she had been accepted she would anyway have stood little chance of being hired by a big corporation on graduation. Female working lives famously followed an M-shaped graph, with large numbers of women leaving their jobs—even being required to—when they got married in their late 20s or early 30s, with some returning later in life to part-time work. Human capital was already thought of as Japan's only real resource in the absence of oil, gas, or precious metals, and one that the country had proved good at developing and nurturing through its well organized and quite egalitarian education system and its in-house corporate training, but this applied only to men.[5] The country passed its first law seeking to enforce equal employment opportunities for women only in 1985.

Thanks to the 1979 Iranian revolution the 1980s had begun with a hike in oil prices, the second inside barely six years. This suddenly raised the input costs of Japanese industry, but exporting companies again proved adept at swiftly regaining their competitiveness, so much so that the country's balance of payments' surplus recovered rapidly, especially its bilateral surplus with its then largest trading partner, the United States. That stubbornly large surplus, at a time of economic and financial strain in a United States that was battling to defeat inflation, gave rise to a long series of 'trade frictions' (*boeki masatsu*) between the United States and Japan during which Japan was forced to accept 'voluntary' restraints on its exports to the US in several sectors as well as listening patiently to demands

---

[5] Miyazawa Kensuke, *Measuring Human Capital in Japan*, RIETI Discussion Paper Series 11-E-037 (2011).

that it make domestic reforms to make its markets more open. The Harley-Davidson motorcycle company became a notable beneficiary of special protection[6] against Japanese imports. Congressmen drew headlines in 1987 by smashing a Toshiba radio on the lawn of the US Capitol, for the benefit of the TV cameras, of course, a stunt repeated in subsequent years with other Japanese products.[7] The deputy US Trade Representative handling some of those negotiations was a lawyer called Robert E. Lighthizer who three decades later returned to public office as President Donald Trump's US Trade Representative, handling similar negotiations with China, over very similar issues. Politically, it was a bumpy decade as relations with the country's closest ally, the United States, were dominated by those so-called frictions. But economically, it was a golden age, one during which Japan seemed to go from strength to strength, especially in comparison to the United States and Western European countries.

It was a golden age during which the statistical measure of Japan's individual wealth, gross domestic product per capita, overtook America's in 1987, helped by the yen's rise in value. It was an age during which Japanese companies exploited that strong currency and easy borrowing terms to buy iconic assets in America, including two Hollywood studios, the Firestone tyre company, Pebble Beach golf course in California, and the Rockefeller Center office building in New York, with Japan's emergence as a huge exporter of capital making it look likely to buy up the world. This was an age during which consumption habits in usually discreet Tokyo became rather conspicuous, famous examples being restaurant dishes with gold leaf sprinkled on rice and a sudden ubiquity in the richer suburbs of fancy foreign cars such as BMWs, Mercedes, and Ferraris. Investors in Japanese equities and property seemed to have found an effortless way to make money. Popular culture reflected this too: in Itami Juzo's satirical film *A Taxing Woman* (*Marusa no Onna*),[8]

---

[6] Kitano Taiju and Ohashi Hiroshi, *Did US Safeguard Resuscitate Harley-Davidson in the 1980s?*, RIETI discussion paper series 07-E-26 (2007): https://www.rieti.go.jp/jp/publications/dp/07e026.pdf.

[7] https://www.washingtonpost.com/archive/opinions/1992/03/08/hammering-americas-image/bdd81faa-7f68-407e-afb9-dbc96baa718a/.

[8] *A Taxing Woman*, directed by Itami Juzo (1987): https://www.imdb.com/title/tt0093502/. Wealth, especially the ill-gotten sort, is a running theme in Itami's films, from a

the female tax inspector who gives the film its title discovers gold bars hidden in a wall in the home of her tax-evader target.

Yet this golden age and all its apparent effortlessness was brought to an end when the Bank of Japan decided in mid-1989 that things were getting dangerously out of hand. To regain control, the central bank tightened monetary conditions by raising its interest rates five times over the subsequent year, which led in turn to an unexpected collapse of stock and property markets that commenced on the first trading day of 1990 and which became the worst financial crash seen in any rich industrialized economy since 1929—until it was outdone in 2008. A banking system that had previously looked invincible, all-powerful, and even supposedly conservative in its lending practices turned out in fact to have been lax and reckless, with part of its capital dependent on now-tumbling stock prices. The bubble had well and truly been burst.

There is room for debate as to whether what then became known as the post-bubble era has yet truly come to an end, although any label applied to a period as long as three decades surely starts to lose its meaning, especially when it refers backwards to the years it followed rather than to any special characteristics of its own. Another popular label, 'the lost decades' is also rather empty in meaning, since the decades certainly occurred and plenty of things happened during them including a fair amount of economic growth. A more helpful way to think about the period is that during as much as a decade and a half the dominant economic force was the financial stress caused by the 1990 crash, even though other forces—such as the rise of new global competition from China, India, and other emerging economies, and an accelerating process of technological change in information and communication industries—were also at work. But later, although the consequences of the financial stress and adjustment to it can still be seen even today, other factors came to be more influential, including demographic change. The surprise, in retrospect, is how long it took for the influence of the crash to fade and be superseded.

Rolls-Royce-owning Buddhist priest in *Funeral* (*Ososhiki*, 1984) to the *yakuza* gangsters depicted in *The Gangster's Moll* (*Minbo*, 1992).

On the surface, what happened was that policy makers and many private companies spent more than half a decade trying to brazen things out in the hope that stock and property markets would eventually recover, bailing out those institutions, companies, and individuals who had lent or borrowed too much. Such an ultimately damaging reliance on wishful thinking destroyed, perhaps forever, the previous image of Japanese bureaucrats as being far-sighted, even omniscient, guardians of the national interest. Then, after that long period of denial, reality eventually struck home in the form of runs on bank deposits and the near collapse of some of the country's biggest financial institutions. Famous names such as Yamaichi Securities and Hokkaido Takushoku Bank disappeared in bankruptcies (both in 1997), while others, including the once-mighty Industrial Bank of Japan, vanished into mergers (in its case, in 2002, when a combination with Dai-Ichi Kangyo Bank and Fuji Bank formed what is now the Mizuho Financial Group), goaded to do so amid belated governmental efforts to clean up the banking system. Despite such efforts, a reluctance to force firms into bankruptcy and to acknowledge losses, assisted by the return to low (soon zero) official interest rates amid an expansionary monetary policy from the Bank of Japan, nevertheless served to keep many unproductive small and medium-sized companies alive, a group which became known as 'zombies',[9] slowing the process of adjustment and recovery. The financial system was saved but damage to the broader, corporate system lingered on. Some big companies, it later turned out, had anyway resorted to accounting fraud in order to try to conceal losses and keep their own shows on the road, even over decades: the most notorious being Olympus, the medical equipment and cameras company, whose fraud was exposed in 2011,[10] and Toshiba, the giant industrial and consumer electronics conglomerate where exposure occurred in 2015.[11]

---

[9] Alan Ahearne and Shinada Naoki, *Zombie Firms and Economic Stagnation in Japan*, Institute of Economic Research, Hitotsubashi University, Hi-Stat Discussion Paper Series (2005): 2. 10.1007/s10368-005-0041-1.

[10] Michael Woodford, *Exposure: Inside the Olympus Scandal* (Portfolio, 2012).

[11] Misawa Mitsuru, *The Toshiba Accounting Scandal: How Corporate Governance Failed*, Asia Case Research Centre, reference 316-0417-1 (2016).

But what was happening under the surface? In summary, the essentials are that during these three decades of *Heisei* Japan became older, the economy became slower-growing as productivity growth also slowed, citizens came to feel more insecure financially and more unequal, and both tertiary education and the workforce became far more female.

* * *

The first of those changes between 1989 and 2019 was also the most substantial and dramatic, though it was quite predictable and widely predicted, at least in its broad direction. This was the transformation in the country's demographic structure, from a nation that had had a fairly young population from 1950 until the 1970s thanks to a huge postwar baby boom into a nation having one of the world's oldest populations—certainly the oldest among big, rich economies. The nation was also transformed from being an expanding one whose population had grown by more than 70 per cent between 1945 and 1989, from 71m people to 123m, to one that since its peak in 2010 of 128m has been shrinking every year and looks destined to continue to do so. As of 2019, the annual rate of population decline was just over 500,000 people.[12]

The change can most easily be illustrated at the extremes. In the late 1980s, as the *Showa* period drew to a close, there were only about 3m Japanese over the age of 80, while around 35m were aged less than 20. Now there are more than 10m people aged over 80 and only around 25m under the age of 20. In 1989, about 2,700 Japanese were over 100 years old. By 2019, the number of centenarians had grown to over 70,000, 90 per cent of them women.[13] That amounts to about one-fifth of the world's total of centenarians and is the world's highest number (4.8 per 10,000 people) relative to population. Italy is the only other big country with a similar centenarian element in its population.

---

[12] *Nippon.com*, 27 December 2019: https://www.nippon.com/en/japan-data/h00624/japan-sees-record-population-decline-in-2019-as-deaths-exceed-births-by-more-than-500–000.html.

[13] *Nippon.com*, 18 September 2019, reporting data from Ministry of Health, Labor, and Welfare: https://www.nippon.com/en/japan-data/h00540/japan's-centenarian-population-tops-70-000.html.

The reasons are by now quite familiar: the emergence of an average life expectancy that at nearly 86 is among the oldest in the world; and of a birth rate that, although far from the world's lowest, at about 1.45 per adult woman is nevertheless well below the replacement rate of 2.1. Given the size of Japan's postwar baby bulge and given a fall in birth rates that became especially noteworthy in the 1990s, this demographic trend was easy to foresee, barring a cataclysm such as war. Moreover, to a large extent the trend was indeed planned for by public and private pension schemes, even if neither birth nor mortality rates are entirely predictable. It was the deteriorating economic environment and its impact on public finances that was unanticipated, rather than the demographics. To judge the sheer magnitude of the change between 1955 and 2015 see Figures 1.1, 1.2, 1.3, and 1.4.

As those figures show, in 1955 by far the largest part of the population was under the age of 30; three decades later in 1985 it was the under 40s that predominated. Now, a further three decades later it is the over 40s, especially those aged between 40 and 65, that are the most numerous, making them also the most influential as voters. It should not be surprising that such a predominant age group is also quite conservative about systemic or institutional change, since they are in their prime working and earning years and so have the most to lose from any redistribution of resources and power.

Perhaps the biggest surprise in demographic terms has been the increase in the number of the extremely old, thanks to the unpredictable long-term effects of healthy diets and of new healthcare technologies. In 1989 a paper[14] by the president of the Institute of Gerontology at Shiraume Women's College in Tokyo projected that the number of Japanese centenarians in 2000 would be 5,400, a seemingly dramatic doubling of the 1989 level. The actual number turned out to be 13,000,[15] a more than quadrupling in just a decade, which was then followed by a further more-than-quintupling to 2019's total of over 70,000.

[14] Hishinuma Shigekazu, *Centenarians in Japan: An Overview, Journal of Insurance Medicine* 21.3 (1989).
[15] Jean-Marie Robine and Saito Yasuhiko, *Survival beyond Age 100: The Case of Japan, Population and Development Review*, Vol 29 (2003).

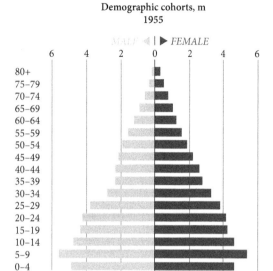

Figure 1.1 Japan's population by age and gender, 1955.
Source: UN Population Division

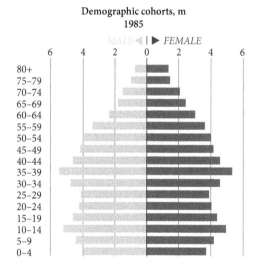

Figure 1.2 Japan's population by age and gender, 1985.
Source: UN Population Division

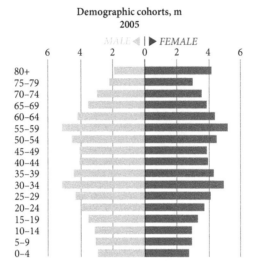

Figure 1.3 Japan's population by age and gender, 2005.
Source: UN Population Division

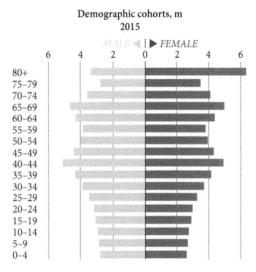

Figure 1.4 Japan's population by age and gender, 2015.
Source: UN Population Division

This transformation of Japan's demographic structure is a sign of success, not failure: of good diet and healthcare, of past economic growth sufficient (so far) to yield the tax revenues and corporate profits to pay for the resulting pensions and healthcare costs. The country's huge public debts somewhat mitigate that joyous interpretation, for recent economic growth has failed to generate a rise in either personal or corporate incomes that is fast enough to be able to generate the tax revenues necessary to be able to start reducing the debt. But as we will see, the debt is easily being financed by a mixture of new borrowing and of monetary creation by the Bank of Japan, so neither pensions nor the health system have come under serious, sustained threat. The more awkward consequence of an ageing society has been the impact on corporate labour costs. Pay and promotion in the typical Japanese corporation are tied to age and seniority, so that as the average employee's age rises, so do wage costs. This has in turn encouraged companies to retain a mandatory retirement age of 60 even as healthy life expectancy has risen: according to the OECD,[16] 80 per cent of companies have stuck to that retirement age, a drop of only ten percentage points over the past decade.

In contrast to some other developed countries, this does not mean that older Japanese people are idle. Japan has one of the highest levels worldwide of participation in the labour force by people over the age of 65. In 2018 nearly a quarter of all over-65s were in work (see Figure 1.5), a proportion more than five times higher than those of Italy or France. This is undoubtedly good for their health as well as meaning that they continue to pay tax. Almost all of these elderly workers, however, are employed part-time or on short-term contracts having been forced to retire from their secure, permanent job at the age of 60. This tends to mean that they are employed in work for which they are over-qualified and in which they receive little or no further training.

The immediate effect of this employment of over-65s is to reduce employers' labour costs below what they would be if they had to stick to seniority and age-based salary structures. What it also does,

---

[16] *OECD Survey of Japan 2019*, fig. 21.

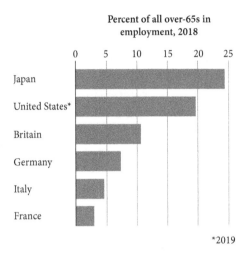

Figure 1.5 Over-65s in employment, selected countries, 2018.
Sources: Eurostat; Statistics Japan

however, is to contribute to a wider and largely detrimental development: the under-use and long-term erosion of the country's human capital. The higher the proportion of the population that is employed on part-time and short-term contracts, the greater the extent of under-employment relative to education and skill levels and to desired amounts and types of work, and the harder it is to increase productivity and hence average earnings. The employment of the elderly is not the largest component of this *Heisei*-era erosion[17] of Japan's human capital, but it is the newest.

*   *   *

The emergence of a highly divided labour market is one of the most important developments of the *Heisei* era. In 1990 approximately 80 per cent of employees enjoyed secure, permanent contracts and only 20 per cent were working on short-term and part-time contracts (see Figure 1.6). Three decades later the proportion on permanent contracts has fallen to slightly above 60 per cent and the proportion on short-term and part-time contracts has nearly doubled to almost

---

[17] *OECD Survey of Japan 2019*, ch. 1 'Labour Market Reform to Cope with a Shrinking and Ageing Population', p. 110.

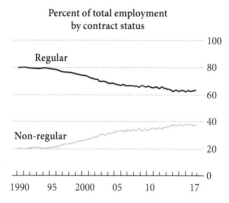

Figure 1.6 Regular and non-regular employment, 1990–2018.
Source: Statistics Japan

40 per cent. This rise of insecurity and erosion of human capital has pushed down wage levels and therefore household incomes and consumption growth. And it has had social effects through its negative impact on the ability or willingness of people, especially the relatively low-skilled, to get married and have children.

Given that until the 1990s Japanese companies were famed for the long-term commitment they made to their employees and for the loyalty and obedience they expected in return, this is quite a radical change. It is not as if the practice known as 'lifetime employment' has disappeared,[18] but rather that it has been modified around the edges in a gradual process of change that has ended up being quite transformative. To understand it, this development needs to be placed in the context of Japan's overall economic performance before and during the *Heisei* era. The bursting of the economic and financial bubble in 1990 represented a marked shift in the country's economic trajectory. During the three decades from 1960 Japan's growth in living standards, measured as GDP per capita, was the fastest in the rich, industrialized world (see Figure 1.7).

The three decades of *Heisei* have, however, seen Japan lose its world champion status. Although all rich countries' growth rates were slower in 1990–2018 than they had been in the immediate

---

[18] *OECD Survey of Japan 2019*, ch. 1, p. 77.

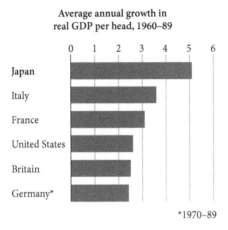

Figure 1.7 Growth in real GDP per head, 1960–89.
Source: World Bank

postwar decades, Japan's annual average growth of GDP per head slipped down the rankings, staying ahead of Italy but falling behind the United States, Britain, France, and Germany (see Figure 1.8). That performance has been a lot better than is implied by the aforementioned label of 'the lost decades' but it nevertheless means that those decades have been meagre by past Japanese standards, thanks to the financial crash that began in 1990.

What never happened following that financial crash was mass unemployment. In contrast to Europe or the United States after their 2008 crash or during earlier recessions, Japan never saw dramatic lay-offs of workers during the 1990s or 2000s. The jobless rate began *Heisei* at slightly above 2 per cent of the workforce and peaked at almost 5.5 per cent in 2002–3 and again in 2009 following the western financial crash. By contrast in 2010 unemployment in the United States peaked at 9.6 per cent. In many EU countries it rose far higher. As 2019 drew to a close, Japan's unemployment rate stood at 2.2 per cent, roughly the same as when *Heisei* had begun. The economic aftermath of the 2020 covid-19 pandemic will raise that unemployment rate sharply once again, but to nowhere near the levels seen in the United States or the EU.

What took place following the bursting of Japan's bubble could be described as the socialization of pain or adjustment, or perhaps

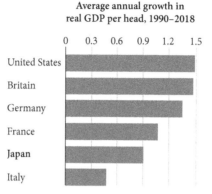

Figure 1.8 Growth in real GDP per head, 1990–2018.
Source: IMF World Economic Outlook Database, April 2019

the social dispersion of pain. Instead of mass firings employers responded by cutting bonuses, overtime, and ultimately wages, and by slowing down and later freezing new hiring. This is the origin of what became the dual labour market, divided between permanent, regular, full-time workers and what the statisticians term non-regular workers, namely those on part-time and temporary contracts or despatched to employers by agencies. Relaxation of labour regulations allowed companies to hire more categories of worker on non-regular terms.

Thanks to the freezes on new hiring, which is reckoned in many companies to have lasted for about a decade, from 1993 until 2004, a disproportionate share of non-regular workers were young people who had the misfortune to graduate from high school and university during that period. The media labelled this 'the ice age generation', and it encompasses about 23 million people born between 1970 and 1982.[19] Not all of those had to enter non-regular jobs—and most women at that time would not have expected permanent employment in any event—but those who did found it hard to move to more permanent contracts once the economy began to improve. The typical Japanese employment system is like a ladder, or perhaps

[19] *Nikkei Asian Review*, 3 August 2019: https://asia.nikkei.com/Spotlight/Comment/Nightmare-2040-Japan-s-lost-generation.

an automated escalator is a better analogy, which if you do not get on at the start is very hard to climb onto later in life.

This shared sacrifice or shared adjustment was undoubtedly a source of social stability. Or it might be argued that Japan's postwar (or, at least, post-1960, when a wave of sometimes violent strikes and protests ceased)[20] social stability was what made this socialization of pain possible. But it has increased both poverty and inequality quite noticeably: according to the OECD,[21] 16 per cent of households live in relative poverty (defined as disposable income lower than 50 per cent of the national median), which is well above the average for OECD member countries. Moreover, that 'relative poverty line' has fallen by 15 per cent in real terms since 1997. Nevertheless, from 2008–18 economic performance did improve somewhat, especially relative to that of other rich industrialized countries (see Figure 1.9). That 2008–18 average was anyway a little depressed by the short-term economic effects of the 2011 earthquake and tsunami that left more than 18,000 people dead or (officially)

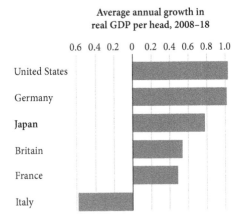

Figure 1.9 Growth in real GDP per head, 2008–18.
Source: IMF World Economic Outlook Database, April 2019

[20] The strike at Mitsui Mining's Miike colliery mine in Kyushu in 1960, which involved violent clashes between tens of thousands of workers, police, and even gangsters, is generally seen as the turning point: John Price, *The 1960 Miike Coal Mine Dispute: Turning Point for Adversarial Unionism in Japan?*, 1991 Bulletin of Concerned Asian Scholars: https://doi.org/10.1080/14672715.1991.10413141.
[21] *OECD Survey of Japan 2017*, pp. 35, 78, 112.

missing and caused a very scary meltdown at the Fukushima Dai-Ichi nuclear plant.

Japan can, therefore, be said to have survived its dramatic financial crash fairly unscathed but nevertheless markedly changed. In terms of economic policy and institutions, the biggest, or at least most striking, change that has occurred has been an almost complete reversal in the role and conduct of the Bank of Japan. This was the institution which triggered the 1990 financial crash by imposing discipline through sharply higher interest rates. In a nod to a worldwide fashion, the government then gave the central bank formal independence through a revised Bank of Japan law in 1997.[22] In the 1990s and 2000s it regularly put pressure on the government to implement economic reforms. Yet since 2013, when the newly elected prime minister, Abe Shinzo, replaced the then governor Shirakawa Masaaki by bringing in a former senior finance ministry official, Kuroda Hirohiko, the central bank has in effect been printing money to finance government spending directly, the very opposite of what 'independence' had been thought to mean. Under the political slogan of 'Abenomics', which consisted of what the prime minister termed the 'three arrows' of fiscal stimulus, monetary expansion, and a limited programme of pro-market structural reform, monetary expansion has done most of the heavy work.

Although all major central banks have engaged in such expansionary policies since the 2008 crash, the Bank of Japan has gone by far the furthest. Whereas assets on the balance sheet of the Federal Reserve Board in America totalled 20 per cent of GDP by the end of 2018 and the European Central Bank's equivalent figure was 40 per cent of Euro-area GDP, the figure for the Bank of Japan was 100 per cent. This effort has made the country's huge public debt—in gross terms, between 1991 and 2018 the general government debt rose from 60 per cent of GDP to 226 per cent,[23] easily the world's largest among rich countries—both affordable and seemingly low-risk. In 2013 the central bank held 10 per cent of outstanding Japanese

---

[22] Jennifer Holt Dwyer, *Explaining Central Bank Reform in Japan*, *Social Science Japan Journal* 7.2 (2004), pp. 245–62: www.jstor.org/stable/30209491.
[23] *OECD Survey of Japan 2019*, 'Key Policy Insights', pp. 21 and 33.

Government Bonds (JGBs); in 2019 its holdings were nearing 50 per cent.[24] It has also become one of the two largest owners of Japanese equities, having by April 2019 bought shares (through vehicles known as Exchange Traded Funds) equivalent to nearly 5 per cent of the market capitalization of the Tokyo Stock Exchange.[25] Such monetary expansion supported the better economic growth of recent years, and is now being mirrored in other central banks' response to the covid-19 pandemic in North America and Europe. But it has not achieved Governor Kuroda's stated objective of ending the country's dozen years of price deflation and of creating an annual rate of increase in consumer prices of about 2 per cent per year.

Despite all sorts of hope and exhortation, wage rises have remained stubbornly modest even as unemployment has fallen, which has in turn limited inflationary pressure. A substantial reason for this has been the prevalence of non-regular employment. As in other advanced countries, Japan has also seen a marked slow-down in productivity growth which has reduced the ability or willingness of companies to raise salaries. This has been a worldwide phenomenon since the 2008 financial crash, but what is surprising in Japan is that it has persisted despite low unemployment and an emerging shortage of labour. In manufacturing, Japanese firms have long been among the earliest and most enthusiastic users of industrial robots and other forms of automation to replace human workers. Yet now, despite still in many ways being at the frontiers of technological development, Japanese companies have not been heavy investors in productivity-enhancing automation, especially in services. Thanks to non-regular employment and the availability of female and elderly workers, labour has remained relatively cheap. And the decline in training that has accompanied the move from regular to non-regular employment has also hindered productivity growth by means of its effect on skill levels and on employees' commitment and work effort.

[24] https://www.reuters.com/article/japan-bonds-boj/rpt-graphic-boj-jgb-buying-lowest-under-kuroda-in-march-as-easing-hits-limits-idUSL3N21G2Q2.
[25] https://asia.nikkei.com/Business/Markets/Bank-of-Japan-to-be-top-shareholder-of-Japan-stocks.

In political terms, the grip on power held by the Liberal Democratic Party was loosened by the crash that began *Heisei* but was broken altogether only briefly in 2009 when the populist Democratic Party of Japan won a landslide election victory, led largely by defectors from the LDP. The DPJ's first prime minister, Hatoyama Yukio, had served as an LDP Diet member from 1986 until leaving to set up a previous new party in 1993. In government, the DPJ made some moves to reallocate public spending away from public works schemes, which were reputed to be corrupt, and towards social welfare, and attempted to reduce the power of the bureaucracy. But a mixture of scandals and incompetence weakened the DPJ, and then its credibility was largely destroyed by its handling of the 2011 tsunami and nuclear meltdown. The DPJ went through three prime ministers[26] inside three years before losing power to the LDP in a Lower House election in December 2012. Politically, Japan was back where it had been ever since the LDP was formed in 1955. And after that revolving-door period of prime ministers, the country then had its longest ever prime ministership, that of Abe Shinzo.

*   *   *

Since the 1990–92 financial crash, only in that 2009 election did voters feel angry enough to choose to support radical changes at national level, although a number of anti-establishment mavericks— actors, comedians, novelists—have been elected at various times as prefectural governors and city mayors. Nevertheless, the sharing of pain has had some noteworthy social consequences which promise to affect the country for decades to come. And that whole process has happened alongside another, more welcome social change, in an arguably surprising correlation, which itself promises to have profound social, economic, and perhaps even political effects during the *Reiwa* era.

For the two most prominent changes—a substantial decline in rates of marriage and in the fertility rate—it is impossible to be sure of the exact causal processes. In both cases, there are likely to be a

---

[26] Hatoyama Yukio, Kan Naoto, and Noda Yoshihiro.

large number of factors at play, interacting with one another in a complex manner, since both marriage and child-rearing are intensely private choices. In what is a strongly family-oriented society, both declines have been surprising, less in their direction than in their extent.

There is an obvious relationship between the two, for although childbirth outside wedlock is not unknown in Japan, it is not widespread and still carries both a social stigma and considerable financial difficulties. For that reason, if fewer people get married it implies that fewer children will be born. And that is what has happened since 1990, on both fronts. Although the proportion of men who reach the age of 50 without ever getting married had been rising slowly during the 1970s and 1980s, the trend accelerated substantially after 1990 (see Figure 1.10). Now a quarter of all 50-year-old men and nearly 15 per cent of women of that age have never been married, and the number is continuing to rise.

The route by which people get married has changed too. As recently as the 1980s, a large proportion of marriages occurred either by being arranged through a formal matchmaker or by a less formal type of matchmaking inside companies. Research[27] by

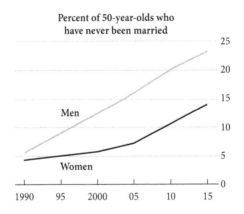

Figure 1.10 Share of men and women never married by age 50.
Source: National Institute for Population and Social Security Research

---

[27] Kato Akihiko, *Declining Marriage and Ever-increasing Childlessness*, Meiji University, 3 October 2018: https://www.meiji.ac.jp/cip/english/research/opinion/Akihiko_Kato.html.

Kato Akihiko and Nakamura Mariko of Meiji University suggests that the prevalence of marriages arranged by formal, informal, and corporate means has fallen from something like 70 per cent in the early 1980s to about 30 per cent now—and most probably within that number fewer of the marriages between corporate colleagues are really any longer 'arranged'.

Meanwhile, the birth rate has also fallen. In all developed countries, wealth, maturity, and social change has led to declining birth rates, generally to below the rate of 2.1 per adult woman that enables a population to replace itself over time. But Japan's decline—like that of some other East Asian countries, including South Korea and Singapore—has gone further than those typical of Western Europe or North America. Figure 1.11 picks out three countries—the United States, France, and Sweden—whose birth rates have stayed closer to the replacement rate than has occurred in Japan. Britain's has also remained at fairly high levels, while Germany's fertility rate has recovered from 1.33 in the mid-2000s to 1.57 in 2019. The European Union's overall fertility rate is currently 1.6, just slightly higher than Germany's.

As in other developed countries, many factors will lie behind this decline in the fertility rate in Japan. But one explanation for the relatively extreme nature of Japan's decline, in a culture in which

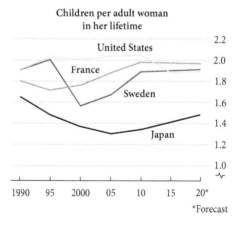

Figure 1.11 Fertility rates, 1990–2020.
Source: UN Population Division

less than 2 per cent of births occur outside marriage, must be the decline in the marriage rate. And among the explanations for the decline in the rate of marriage, the state of the economy and in particular of the labour market ranks highly.[28] Marriage and child-rearing require resources and some sense of security. In the newly divided labour market, men who are able only to find non-regular employment contracts can offer neither resources nor security as a family's traditional breadwinner. This applied notably to the 'ice age generation' entering work and the prime marriage years during the 1990s and 2000s, and especially the lower skilled. Men, particularly in lower social classes, have found it harder than in the past to get married and start a family. It is not coincidental that during the same decades a new phenomenon emerged among middle-aged, predominantly single men: the 'otaku' or geek, who devotes much of their leisure time to such pastimes as video gaming or joining fan groups following teenage female pop idols.[29]

Professor Kato of Meiji University argues[30] that the link between the declining earning power of the lower skilled and a declining marriage rate can be traced back as far as the 1970s. But it has accelerated during the 1990s and 2000s thanks to the spread of non-regular employment contracts. As he writes,[31] lack of resources is the key issue preventing marriages in a society in which:

> …according to the survey by the National Institute of Population and Social Security Research, even today, 90% of the never-married persons in their late 20s said they 'intend to marry someday'. When asked what the biggest obstacle is, 'money for marriage' came out as the top answer for both men and women, accounting for as much as 50%.

At the same time, one of the biggest developments in the labour market has been the large rise, especially rapid in the years 2012–19,

[28] Kato Akihiko, *Two Major Factors behind the Marriage Decline in Japan: The Deterioration in Macroeconomic Performance and the Diffusion of Individualism Ideology*, paper delivered at Population Association of America Annual Meeting 2012: https://paa2012.princeton.edu/abstracts/121688. Also published in *Journal of Population Problems* 67.2 (2011).

[29] Portrayed vividly and memorably in a documentary by Miyake Kyoko, *Tokyo Idols* (2017), broadcast by BBC Four and NHK: https://kyokomiyake.com/tokyo-idols.

[30] Kato, 2012.   [31] Kato, 2018.

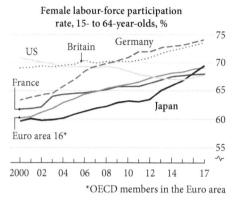

Female labour-force participation
rate, 15- to 64-year-olds, %

*OECD members in the Euro area

Figure 1.12 Female employment rate, 15–64-year-olds, 2000–17.
Source: OECD

in the number of women going out to work. During 2015, the proportion of prime working age women (i.e. between 15 and 64 years old) who are active in the labour force overtook the level in the United States (where the participation rates for both men and women were declining). This places Japanese female labour-force participation in the 15–64 age bracket at roughly the same level as in the euro area countries, but still about 4–5 percentage points lower than in Britain and Germany (see Figure 1.12). Female participation rates are even higher in Sweden and Switzerland.

The Japanese government's view about this rise in female working is that it is a result of policies aimed at women's 'empowerment', initiated by Prime Minister Abe soon after he re-entered[32] office in 2012 and stated that he wanted Japan to be a country in which 'women shine'.[33] It is true that the Abe government, in collaboration with local governments, has spent much more on providing public childcare facilities, adding 530,000 childcare places and 300,000 more after-school-care places in 2013–17, according to the OECD.[34] However, while it is clear that an impressive increase in the quantity

---

[32] Abe Shinzo's first term as prime minister lasted just one year, in 2006–7.
[33] The phrase was first used by PM Abe in a speech on 22 January 2014 at the World Economic Forum in Davos, Switzerland: https://japan.kantei.go.jp/96_abe/statement/201401/22speech_e.html. He continued to return to the theme for several years afterwards: see e.g. PM Abe's speech on 27 September 2015 to a Global Leaders Meeting on Gender Equality and Female Empowerment: https://www.mofa.go.jp/files/000101698.pdf.
[34] *OECD Survey of Japan*, p. 19.

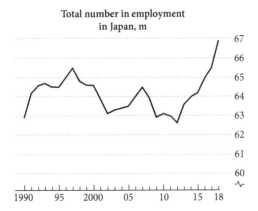

Figure 1.13 Japan's employed population, 1990–2018.
Source: Haver Analytics

of female work has occurred, assisted by such childcare investment, it is less clear that there has been any commensurate improvement in the quality of female work, which is what empowerment or shining would surely imply.

This increase in the propensity of women to go out to work has contributed, alongside the previously discussed rise in the employment of men aged 65 and over, to a remarkable rise in Japan's total employed population (see Figure 1.13). This has been particularly marked since 2012, when the economy began to recover from the shock caused by the 2011 tsunami and nuclear meltdown. It is remarkable because it has been happening at the same time as the overall population has been declining. Indeed, the working-age (15–64) population has fallen by 12 per cent since 2000.

So increased employment of working-age women and retired people of both genders has more than made up for population decline. But about half of the 2.5 million-strong rise in female employment since 2013 has come from non-regular forms of work.[35] Only 45 per cent of women have regular contracts compared with 78 per cent for men (a male figure which declined during the 'ice age' period but has since risen again). Women account for two-thirds of non-regular workers, where their share of the population

---

[35] *OECD Survey of Japan 2019*, p. 91.

would imply that in an equitable system they would account for only half. In 2017 the share of women working for less than 30 hours per week was 37 per cent, well above the OECD average of 25 per cent. Not surprisingly, the gender wage gap remains the third highest in the OECD, though it has declined from 33 per cent in 2005 to 25 per cent in 2017.

It should be noted that at the same time as financial stress and the rise of non-regular work has depressed the marriage rate, and as an oncoming labour shortage has raised the employment rate for both working-age women and retired people, the number of dual-income households has also soared. Dual-income households overtook the number of conventional single-earner households (i.e. containing a working husband and non-working wife) in the mid-1990s;[36] there are now roughly twice as many dual-income households as conventional single-earner households, but there are also a lot more single-person households too. Changing social norms about work and family will have contributed to this, but economic pressures too. The same decline in incomes and the sense of security that lies behind the decline in marriage and fertility rates lies behind much of the increase in female non-regular work and dual-income households.

These economic pressures are, however, what also makes the final social change to be noted in this chapter especially surprising. This is the decision by girls graduating from high school to attend four-year university courses in dramatically increasing numbers, throughout the 1990s and 2000s. During the 1970s and 1980s, the gender gap in full, four-year tertiary education was huge, with all but 10–12 per cent of 18-year-old girls going on to study at two-year junior colleges or not at all, while 35–40 per cent of their male contemporaries were going to university (see Figure 1.14). There is still a gender gap of about five percentage points, but nevertheless half of female high-school graduates now attend four-year university courses.

In the generation that graduated during the 1980s and are now in or entering leadership positions in organizations there was therefore only a small pool of female candidates, but in subsequent generations the pipeline of university-educated women is going to be

---

[36] *OECD Survey of Japan 2019*, p. 91.

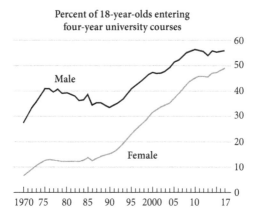

Percent of 18-year-olds entering
four-year university courses

Figure 1.14 University entrants by gender, 1970–2017.
Source: MEXT

much, much larger. Among so-called millennials, those born after 1980 and who therefore graduated from university after 2000, the numbers of professional females will be especially large. Someone who entered university in 2000 was by 2019 only about 37 years old. Most Japanese organizations stick quite rigidly to promoting by age and seniority. The current lack of women in leadership positions— only about 13 per cent of managerial roles in Japan were occupied by women in 2019[37]—reflects the huge past gender gap in tertiary education, as well no doubt as other barriers. Among the millennials, the tertiary education gender gap will play a far smaller role.

*   *   *

As Japan moved during 2019 from *Heisei* to *Reiwa*, under the new reign of Emperor Naruhito, it was a country that had moved not exactly from triumph to disaster—though there had been disasters and near-disasters along the way—but rather from economic outperformance to a sort of steady mediocrity. As all those 70,000-plus centenarians show, it is a country that has become markedly older and is in many ways a pioneer worldwide in coming to terms with an ageing population. It is a country in which despite virtually continuous handwringing about whether its education system is fit for

---

[37] *OECD Survey of Japan 2019*, p. 103.

purpose nevertheless continues to rank highly in the OECD's standardized test rankings[38] and, as Figure 1.14 demonstrated, is sending 50–60 per cent of its young men and women to full university courses.

Yet Japan is also a country in which a deeply divided labour market has produced detrimental outcomes: stubbornly depressed real incomes and hence depressed household consumption and savings as well worsened conditions for marriage and family formation; and a deterioration in the development and use of human capital, as a large proportion of the workforce is employed in jobs below their level of education and skills and without the sort of in-house corporate training and development that their (mainly male) forebears enjoyed. Productivity growth has shrunk dramatically, particularly thanks to a widening divergence between the most productive firms and the least, a divergence which is not being cleared up by the disappearance of those firms through acquisition or bankruptcy.[39] Poverty and inequality have increased—not quite to the high levels that exist in America, but they have increased nevertheless. The result is that a country that could and arguably should be a high-wage, high-quality place, operating at or near the technology frontier—a sort of much larger Asian version of Switzerland—enters *Reiwa* as a surprisingly low-wage, even high poverty society. It doesn't look like that if you wander the streets of central Tokyo. But it is.

At the same time, however, Japan has entered *Reiwa* as an increasingly female place. Not that there are any more females than in the past, of course, but rather that thanks to the shrinking population and to the surge of female access to university education in the 1990s and 2000s women are actively competing for roles they could barely have dreamt of in previous decades. Whether its men like it or not—and in a still misogynistic society, many do not—Japan is destined to have a far more female future. The question is whether it will embrace that future to anything close to its full potential.

---

[38] *OECD PISA Tests 2018*: https://www.oecd.org/pisa/publications/PISA2018_CN_JPN.pdf.
[39] *OECD Survey of Japan 2017*, pp. 79–85.

2

A Place Where Women Shine?[1]

To understand the extent to which Japan remains a particularly
male-dominated, misogynistic society, a good place to start is with
the fact that the oral contraceptive pill was not authorized for use in
Japan until 1999.[2] This was a full thirty-nine years after the Food
and Drug Administration approved its use in the United States,
an approval followed swiftly in Western European countries. And
when the pill was finally authorized, the catalyst for the decision
was actually the authorization of Viagra, at a record speed for a
foreign drug, which led to protests about the disparity of treatment
between men and women. The 'morning after' contraceptive pill
remains available only on a doctor's prescription. There are certainly many cultural factors affecting choices of contraception in
every country and many vested interests at play in authorization
decisions, and what is also unusual about Japan in terms of birth
control has long been the ready availability of abortions, which
were legalized and normalized many years before such developments occurred in most western countries.[3] But it is undeniable
that one important factor behind the very belated official authorization of the contraceptive pill was male domination of the medical
profession, of drug authorization procedures, and of public discourse in the media and elsewhere about birth control.

A second good place to look is therefore the scandal in 2018 at
Tokyo Medical University (TMU), a privately run but prestigious

---

[1] The phrase in the official English version used in Prime Minister Abe's speech to the
World Economic Forum on 22 January 2014 in Davos, Switzerland: https://japan.kantei.
go.jp/96_abe/statement/201401/22speech_e.html.
[2] Analia Vitale, *The Unpopular Contraceptive Pill: Birth Control and Gender in the Japanese
Press*, *U.S.-Japan Women's Journal* 29 (2005), pp. 60–76: www.jstor.org/stable/42771935.
[3] Abortion was legalized by the 1948 Eugenic Protection Law.

college. In that year it emerged[4] that TMU had been systematically discriminating against female applicants in order to achieve a target proportion of graduating male doctors. The apparent grounds for this discrimination was a belief that female doctors are liable to take long periods of maternity leave and even to leave the profession altogether once they have children, so if the necessary number of doctors was to be maintained it was thought best to ensure that a disproportionate number of medical students are men. It later transpired, following investigation by the Ministry of Education, Culture, Sports, and Technology (officially abbreviated as MEXT), that at least nine other medical universities were also manipulating the exam scores of female applicants in a similar way. TMU responded in the traditional manner with deep-bowing apologies and resignations of its top executives, and remarkably quickly after the scandal managed to elect its first female president from among its faculty. It also began to compensate female applicants who had lost out from this manipulation over the previous two years (although the practice was found to date back to at least a decade earlier).

This TMU scandal tells us three main things, one negative and two positive. The negative point is unfortunately the most important: this is that the medical schools are serving an employment system in the universal public healthcare service that is itself rather rigid and discriminatory against women. If the government truly wishes to intervene to empower women then one would have imagined it might have thought of doing so in the case of a massive employer that it regulates directly,[5] but evidently not. In many countries, medicine has been one of the fields in which women have progressed quite rapidly. Among the thirty-six largely wealthy member countries of the OECD, on average 47 per cent of doctors were female in 2017; in Scandinavia, Eastern Europe, and the Baltic

---

[4] G. Wheeler, *The Tokyo Medical University Entrance Exam Scandal: Lessons Learned*, *Int J Educ Integr* 14 (2018).

[5] Japan's universal public health system is a mixed service financed by mandatory insurance along with patient fees and government subsidies, regulated by national and local government, but provided by private and non-profit entities as well as some hospitals directly owned and run by national or local government. See *International Health Care System Profiles*, The Commonwealth Fund: *https://international.commonwealthfund.org/countries/japan/*.

States, often between 50–70 per cent of doctors are women. But in Japan only 20 per cent of doctors are women. Although that was at least a rise from 14 per cent in 2000, it leaves the Japanese ratio the lowest in the whole OECD.[6]

Tuition fees for medicine are very high and it takes six years of study to qualify, but both of those points are also true in other countries. It is the health-service's employment practices which have failed to adapt sufficiently to allow it to recruit and retain those female doctors who also wish to have children. The medical colleges have therefore been discriminatory in service of a discriminatory health service. In that, the health system echoes a general point about employment practices in Japanese organizations: too many have remained rigidly male-oriented, demanding long working hours, very limited holidays or other absences, and a degree of commitment or obligation which makes it even harder for Japanese women to combine careers and families than it is for their equivalents elsewhere. In a nutshell, this tells us what needs to change in all kinds of organizations if women are to 'shine'.

Yet let us also look on the brighter side. The first of the two positive messages from the TMU scandal is that it shows that increasing numbers of women have been applying to study medicine and have been doing well enough in the examinations to force the misogynistic admissions staff to fiddle the results. That looks to be why the manipulations date back only a decade or so; before then fiddling presumably wasn't thought necessary. The second positive message is that rather than just being shrugged off as business as usual the TMU scandal caused something of a national outcry. Amid the outcry, a group of women even sued the university for compensation for having been rejected unfairly.[7] It was probably not coincidental that the following year, Japan's top national university, the University of Tokyo,[8] chose to invite a leading female scholar of feminism and

---

[6] *OECD Survey of Japan 2019*, p. 104.

[7] https://english.kyodonews.net/news/2018/10/ab5c98af63ae-women-demand-tokyo-medical-univ-compensate-over-entry-exam-rigging.html.

[8] Disclosure: since 2006, I have served on the University of Tokyo's international advisory council, now known as its Global Advisory Board. Starting in 2019, I am also an 'Ushioda Fellow' at the university's new inter-disciplinary research institute, Tokyo College.

gender equality, Professor Ueno Chizuko (who was for many years a professor at the university) to give its annual matriculation address to its incoming students.[9]

The speech was remarkably tough and frank about the discrimination that especially the female students should expect to face, building on the scandal at Tokyo Medical University. But Professor Ueno also spared no blushes at the University of Tokyo itself, an institution in which as she said:

> ...female students are approximately 20% of undergraduates, 25% in master's programs, and 30.7% in doctoral programs. When they step into academia, among scholars, women are 18.2% among assistant professors, 11.6% among associate professors, and only 7.8% among professors. This percentage is lower than those of women politicians in Parliament. Women deans are one out of fifteen, and there has been no woman president to this date.

At Harvard University female students are about 49 per cent of undergraduates while in 2018 more women were admitted as undergraduates at Oxford than men for the first time. Harvard had its first female president in 2007 (Drew Gilpin Faust) and Oxford its first female vice-chancellor in 2016 (Louise Richardson). Tokyo and other national public universities are well behind the top private universities (such as Keio, Doshisha, and Waseda) in raising their levels of female students and faculty: in the top five national universities, 24 per cent of undergraduates are female whereas in the top five private universities 44 per cent are female.[10] Tokyo's proportion of female undergraduate students has essentially flatlined for the past decade.

Such willingness to speak out and, in the University of Tokyo's case, to provide a platform for such discourse is the second positive finding from the TMU scandal. Other recent stories also illustrate the fairly new willingness of Japanese women to fight back against

---

[9] English version of Professor Ueno Chizuko's speech delivered on 12 April 2019 in Japanese, published by Women's Action Network, the NGO she now leads: https://wan.or.jp/article/show/8348.

[10] *The Power of Parity: Advancing Women's Equality in Asia-Pacific*, McKinsey Global Institute (2018), p. 164.

discrimination and the extent of the barriers that they face. A harrowing but brave case is that of a young journalist, Ito Shiori, who in December 2019 won a civil case[11] in the Tokyo District Court for damages she claimed against a prominent, well-connected male TV journalist, Yamaguchi Noriyuki, for a 2015 rape which prosecutors had chosen not to pursue on grounds of insufficient evidence. After that refusal to prosecute, Ito-san went public about the alleged assault rather than keeping quiet about it, and in 2017 even published a book, *Black Box*, about the event. Although Ito-san has been widely vilified in traditional and social media, as is often the lot of female complainants worldwide, her book won an award from the Free Press Association of Japan in 2018.

Another instance is the battle against a less dramatic but still discriminatory practice, that of companies and other organizations laying down dress codes for female employees that are essentially designed to make women decorative at work rather than functional. Ishikawa Yumi, a temporary (i.e non-regular contract) worker who is also an actress and writer, in 2019 sparked off a social-media campaign against the mandatory wearing of high heels by female employees in many workplaces which drew quite strong public support.[12] Ishikawa- san then trained her social-media fire on other discriminatory or demeaning corporate rules, such as a ban on women wearing glasses or requirements to wear make-up.[13] In a culture in which not rocking the boat is a basic principle taught from elementary school onwards, such questioning of what are seen as outdated practices represents a potentially significant change of mood and of direction.

*   *   *

As in every country, the case for rooting out this sort of gender discrimination in Japan must primarily be one based on justice and human rights, rather than economics. The huge gap in women's de facto rights and freedom of choice compared with the rights and

---

[11] https://www.japantimes.co.jp/news/2019/12/18/national/crime-legal/japan-journalist-shiori-ito-wins-rape-case/#.XgDOti2cYjc.

[12] https://www.nytimes.com/2019/12/10/world/asia/japan-kutoo-high-heels.html.

[13] https://www.bbc.com/news/business-50342714.

choice available to men is by far Japan's biggest case of social injustice, simply thanks to the number of people involved.

The legal, de jure, rights of men and women have been made more or less equal through a series of laws[14] beginning with formal equality under the law for the first time in 1946; the Equal Employment Opportunity Law in 1985; a Childcare Leave law in 1991; a so-called Basic Law for a Gender Equal Society in 1999; and a Law for the Prevention of Spousal Violence in 2001. In addition, in 2015 the Diet passed the 'Act on Promotion of Women's Participation and Advancement in the Workplace' which required any organization of more than three hundred employees to publish data on their gender diversity as well as 'diversity action plans'. In addition, the Ministry of Health, Labour, and Welfare instituted a certification scheme to recognize companies thought to have especially good procedures for promoting female participation.

Japan is even rated[15] as offering the most generous rights for paternity leave in the world under that 1991 law and subsequent amendments, as in principle paid childcare leave can be taken by either mothers or fathers during their baby's first year, with incomes maintained either by the government or the company at 80 per cent of the parents' normal income. Fathers can split their time off into two parts. But very few fathers—just over 6 per cent in 2018—actually take it up,[16] citing work-place culture and working style as their main excuses. In fact, in 2019 a number of fathers who did take up those rights ended up taking out lawsuits against their employers alleging discrimination against them for having done so.[17]

As is shown by that example of paternity leave, as well as by the efforts by Ito Shiori and Ishikawa Yumi cited above, it is the way in which institutions implement or impede rights and choices where

[14] List cited in *Gender and Equality in Japan*, a presentation by Bando Mariko, Chancellor of Showa Women's University, 12 October 2016.
[15] *Nippon.com*, 25 July 2019: https://www.nippon.com/en/japan-data/h00500/japan-has-the-best-paternity-leave-system-but-who's-using-it.html.
[16] Matsukawa Rui, *Mandatory Paternity Leave Is the Key to Womenomics*, Association of Japanese Institutes for Strategic Studies 21, 20 December 2019: http://www2.jiia.or.jp/en_commentary/pdf/AJISS-Commentary281.pdf.
[17] *Japan Times*, 16 September 2019: https://www.japantimes.co.jp/news/2019/09/16/national/social-issues/japan-paternity-leave-suit-rights/#.XgTvPS2cZMM.

the gap lies and where the social injustice is rooted. The de jure rights are fine; it is the de facto ones that are not.

This social injustice has economic consequences, too: the institutional obstruction of women's rights and choice is a big part of the reason why Japan's economy has lagged so badly in terms of productivity growth, for organizations are using many employees, but especially female ones, in inefficient ways, with women performing tasks that are below their capabilities and men forced to work long but unproductive hours and so to sacrifice work–life balance or family roles. If the country is, to repeat Prime Minister Abe's 2014 words, genuinely to become a place in which 'women shine',[18] a wide range of things need to be changed by institutions of all kinds, many of which would have the welcome side effect of raising productivity and so boosting the economy and living standards. Although to seek what we might call the more effective use of human capital may sound technical and even mercenary, it means the same thing as giving women the chance to fulfil their potentials in any way they wish to. That is the only thing that 'shining' can really mean.

One change that has already begun to occur, however, is a necessary precursor to that transformation: Japan has become a place in which women have shown that they want to be able to shine, in all sorts of ways. Before the Pacific war, when Japan's economy was still quite rural, women had a high level of participation in the labour force while also raising and running their families. It was during the five decades after 1945 when this changed, in a much more urban, industrializing country, to a prevailing division of labour in which men went out to work, in what steadily became conditions of lifetime employment on permanent contracts, while most women stayed at home to take responsibility for the family. That was reflected in the big gender gap in tertiary education seen as recently as the 1980s, a time when families still believed it was not worth sending their daughters to university. As Figure 1.14 showed, in 1983 just 12.2 per cent of girls graduating from high school went on to four-year university courses compared with 36.1 per cent of boys of that same age group. In 1990, when the bubble economy burst,

---

[18] Abe, Davos 2014.

still only 15.2 per cent of girls went on to four-year courses, less than half as many as boys. But by a decade later, in 2000, the girls' figure had doubled, to 31.5 per cent, while the boys' share had risen to 47.5 per cent. And in 2010 the girls' figure had risen sharply again, to 45.2 per cent while boys had reached 56.4 per cent. The girls' number is now approaching 50 per cent. Given Japan's shrinking population of young people, what this means in absolute numbers is that in 1983 roughly 110,000 female high-school graduates went on to four-year university courses, while in 2010 roughly 280,000 such young females went on to four-year courses.

Consequently, there has now emerged a generation of women, mainly still aged in their 30s and 40s, that have the ability and the desire to take up influential roles of all kinds, in organizations big and small, grand and humble, all around the country. This is the first time in Japanese history when this has occurred. It remains a phenomenon of potentiality more than actuality. Nevertheless Bando Mariko, who is now president of Showa Women's University and who during her thirty-four-year career as a bureaucrat and policy advisor was an important and active campaigner for greater gender equality, thinks[19] that this greater supply of female graduates coming through the career pipeline means that the share of section chiefs and more senior managers who are female will at least double over the next ten years. This would raise the share of female managers up to about 25 per cent: still low but moving quite strongly in the right direction and creating a critical mass of female influence in managerial decision-making.

Bando-san was a rare female student at Tokyo University in 1965, a time when only 3 per cent of undergraduates there were female. She studied literature and says that in her classes, the women were all outstanding, whereas the larger number of men ranged much more widely in their levels of ability. But when she graduated, private companies made no job offers to the female graduates at all. That is why she joined the government. Now a widely read writer, Bando-san's belief is that female empowerment has passed through three critical stages in Japan: first, protection for women under the

---

[19] Interview at Showa Women's University, Tokyo, 6 December 2016.

postwar labour laws; second, the equal opportunity law of 1985; third, the expansion of publicly subsidized childcare; and now the country is in the fourth stage, one during which, she hopes, women will be encouraged to fulfil their abilities.

If Bando-san's prediction comes true and the female role continues to grow in subsequent decades this would, as in other countries, still leave men with a level of influence and leadership that is vastly disproportionate to their roughly 50 per cent share in the population, but it would place large numbers of women alongside them for the first time in history. Meanwhile, the ageing and gradual shrinking in the country's total population mean that more and more organizations are coming to realize that they need to adapt their ways of working and behaving in order not just to accommodate more women but also actively to attract them. This has the potential to accelerate the process.

Plainly, the struggle is an uphill one. On virtually any measure, Japan lags well behind other advanced, wealthy countries in terms of gender equality: on the simplest index-based ranking that synthesizes a wide range of data, the World Economic Forum's annual *Global Gender Gap Report*,[20] Japan has a lowly ranking that even keeps on slipping as other countries make more progress: in the 2020 report, using 2019 data, Japan slipped eleven places from 110th to 121st out of 153 countries placing it ignominiously between the United Arab Emirates and Kuwait. Admittedly both South Korea (108th) and China (106th) also score poorly, but you have to go way up the rankings to find another big, wealthy country: Italy in 76th place. In politics in 2017 women made up just 10 per cent of members of the Lower House of Parliament but just over 20 per cent of the less powerful Upper House; they fare even worse in regional and local government, with 6.4 per cent of Prefectural Governorships, 9.9 per cent of seats in Prefectural Assemblies, and just 2.3 per cent of city mayors.[21]

Any improvement will come from a very poor starting point. That said, there are some important signs of change, beyond simply the rise in the quantity of work being done by women. Kathy

---

[20] World Economic Forum Global Gender Gap Report 2020, published 2019: https://www.weforum.org/reports/gender-gap-2020-report-100-years-pay-equality.

[21] Cabinet Office data.

Matsui, a vice-chairman at Goldman Sachs in Tokyo, has been overseeing studies on what she termed 'womenomics' in Japan since 1999, arguing that a much fuller and more productive role for women has the potential to boost annual economic output by as much as 10–15 per cent. When her first report was published, labour-force participation of women aged 15–64 was just 56 per cent; now, as mentioned earlier, it has risen to beyond 70 per cent. But there is a new mood, too. In her latest report,[22] published in 2019, she and her colleagues wrote that:

> As a result of widespread labour shortages and a growing economy, there is a growing realization that gender diversity in the workplace is no longer an option, but an economic and business imperative.

Moreover, Goldman Sachs argued that it is an imperative that can be shown to pay off. Now that, under the 2015 legislation, larger companies are being required to disclose their gender statistics, the report was able to show that among the 297 Japanese listed firms that disclosed their numbers of female managers in the June 2018–April 2019 period, those that had 15 per cent or more female managers also boasted the highest five-year average sales growth and the highest three-year average returns on equity.

Diversity has become a fashionable mantra in corporate Japan. In May 2019 a Japanese chapter was even established of an organization that originated in Britain in 2010 called 'The 30 per cent Club'.[23] This organization is dedicated to promoting gender balance on corporate boards and in senior management, using a target of 30 per cent female board directors and 30 per cent female senior managers. When the UK campaign was launched in 2010 the proportion of female directors at FTSE 100 listed companies was 12.5 per cent, but the group's 30 per cent target was exceeded during 2018 and by December 2019 the level had reached 32.7 per cent.[24] For the new Japanese chapter, the starting point is not too dissimilar: for TOPIX

---

[22] '20 Years On, Womenomics 5.0: Progress, Areas for Improvement, Potential 15% GDP Boost', Goldman Sachs Portfolio Strategy Research, 15 April 2019.
[23] https://30percentclub.org/about/who-we-are.
[24] https://30percentclub.org/about/chapters/united-kingdom.

100 listed companies (i.e. the largest or most valuable on the Tokyo Stock Exchange), the proportion of female board directors in July 2019 was 10.5 per cent, which was 2.5 percentage points higher than in the previous year and far higher than the 4 per cent level seen in 2014.[25]

This realization that gender diversity is both necessary and beneficial has been a long time coming, primarily because labour shortages have themselves been a long time coming. Thanks to demographic trends they have been widely predicted for years, but slower than expected economic growth along with the availability of pools of cheap, non-regular contract labour among women and retirees have kept on deferring the seemingly inevitable. But the crunch finally hit in 2018–19, forcing employers and the government to confront a choice between permitting increased immigration and fostering a greater role for women. There will be some increased immigration: Goldman Sachs reckons[26] that already in 2018 an influx of foreign workers, mainly technical trainees and people on student visas, made up 15 per cent of the total growth in employees (182,000 out of 1.2 million), and a new visa programme enacted in late 2018 will permit, from April 2019, an expected 345,000 foreign workers to move to Japan over the next five years to work in specified sectors. Such an increase in immigration, from its current low base (only around 2 per cent of the population is foreign-born, compared with levels ranging from 10–25 per cent in Western Europe and North America), would still leave a wide opportunity for women. The economic effect of the 2020 global covid-19 pandemic may be to delay this opportunity once again, but it will not alter the demographic reality.

∗   ∗   ∗

It is largely institutions that need to change if this opportunity is to be grasped, more than laws. But there remain two laws in particular which obstruct change: those for tax and immigration.

---

[25] *Nikkei Asian Review*, 29 October 2019, article by Kobayashi Nobuko, an Ernst & Young Japan partner: https://asia.nikkei.com/Opinion/Gender-diversity-in-Japan-Inc.-must-blast-past-tokenism.
[26] Goldman Sachs (2019), pp. 7–8.

Currently, a spousal deduction from a married couple's income tax acts as a disincentive for women to do more than work part-time. Under the law, a normal household's primary earner benefits from a Y380,000 deduction from their income tax if there is a secondary earner who brings in less than Y1.5 million a year. By normal is meant a primary earner bringing in up to Y11.2 million a year, which is more than double the average household income of Y5.1 million. The amount deducted from the primary earner's income tax is reduced in stages as the secondary earner's income rises towards Y2.01 million, and then above that is lost altogether. The deduction is also reduced according to a formula if the primary earner's income rises to Y12.2 million and then is unavailable to higher earners.

It's complicated, like all income tax thresholds and rules. There are also thresholds for pension premiums and healthcare insurance to be taken into account. The key point however is that what the tax and social security rules do is to offer some benefit to households who get a bit of extra income if the wife does some part-time work at or close to the minimum wage, but then penalizes the household through quite a sharp rise in taxation if she chooses to work longer or for higher pay. This tax and social security system dates back to the 1960s when most households had a single earner. In 2016 the spousal deduction was expected to be abolished and replaced with a standard deduction for all married couples, regardless of income, but with elections coming up the Liberal Democratic Party's tax commission decided instead just to raise the secondary earner's income entitlement from the previous Y1.03 million to Y1.5 million. On paper that was an impressive nearly 50 per cent rise but it is one that still leaves a big tax penalty in place for any spouse wanting to do more than minimum-wage work. It looks more like a gesture than a real reform.[27] It left the tax and social security system still reflecting the Japan of the 1960s rather than the twenty-first century. Such archaic thinking was also evident during the covid-19 pandemic in the spring of 2020: when the government made a cash

---

[27] Morinobu Shigeki, a former finance ministry official now at Chuo University, gave the reform a 'mixed grade': *Nippon.com*, 12 January 2017: https://www.nippon.com/en/currents/d00280/a-mixed-grade-for-japans-new-tax-reform-plan.html.

payment of Y100,000 available to every citizen in order to make up for lost earnings or other suffering, the system adopted meant that only heads of households were eligible to complete the application, which necessarily normally meant men. Husbands were expected to apply on behalf of their wives. "Shining" and equality were in effect suspended.

There is one possible explanation for this glaring gap between the shining women rhetoric and the decisions of the LDP on tax and welfare. This is that some influential, conservative elements within the ruling party do not in fact believe in the rhetoric and instead believe women should still be incentivized to stay at home and raise children. Prime Minister Abe and virtually all senior figures in the party are members of an association called Nippon Kaigi, normally translated as 'Japan Conference', which Professor Jeffrey Kingston, Director of Asia Studies at Temple University in Japan, describes in a recent book[28] as 'a right-wing lobby organisation known for its support of traditional values and patriotism'. This quite shadowy network or organization, which was created only in 1997 through mergers between previous lobby groups, is mainly known for its promotion of historical revisionism (i.e. a benign, even positive view of Japan's imperial expansion and military conduct between 1895 and 1945), of reforming the pacifist clauses of the constitution, and of protecting the imperial system.[29] But amidst those traditional values there exists considerable scepticism about whether gender equality really suits Japan.

Against that sense of latent hypocrisy in the ruling party does have to be placed the government's genuine investment in childcare facilities. As Goldman Sachs's report[30] notes, total daycare capacity has expanded by 27 per cent between 2012 and 2018, from 2.2 million places nationwide to 2.8 million, beating the rise in demand during that period and as a result reducing the number of wait-listed children from nearly 25,000 in 2012 to 19,900 by April 2018. Corporate and other institutional investment in childcare facilities has also

---

[28] Jeff Kingston, *Japan* (Polity Press, 2019), p. 45.
[29] Yoshifumi Tawara, *What Is the Aim of Nippon Kaigi, the Ultra-Right Organization That Supports Japan's Abe Administration?*, Asia-Pacific Journal Japan Focus, 1 November 2017.
[30] Goldman Sachs (2019), p. 14.

grown substantially during this period. This has lowered—though far from eliminated—one of the barriers to combining career and family. It has not led to an increase in the number of births each year, which have continued to decline,[31] nor has it yielded any sustained improvement in the total fertility rate.[32]

More evidence of hypocrisy, or at least of conflicting priorities, comes in the new immigration law.[33] One of the main ways in which working mothers in other advanced countries have reconciled child-rearing with arduous professional work schedules has been by hiring domestic help of various kinds: nannies, au pairs, cleaners, or often all three. Given the country's labour shortage, it is hard and expensive to hire Japanese nannies. But although foreign expatriates in Japan are permitted to bring foreign nannies or other domestic help with them, this is not possible for Japanese citizens. The new 2018 immigration law relaxed visa requirements for some categories of caregivers so as to ease shortages in nursing, but not for domestic help. Hiring Filipino, Indonesian, or Chinese nannies keen on learning or improving their Japanese language skills might be mainly something that wealthier households would be able to afford, yet to permit it would surely harm nobody and would widen the scope of childcare provision in such a way as to ease some pressure on publicly funded facilities.

*   *   *

More deep-set obstacles to improving households' ability to reconcile family and careers can be found in the workplace and the way in which companies are organized. As noted in Chapter 1, traditionally a graph of Japanese women's working lives was shaped like an 'M', with high participation in work before marriage but then a big drop-out rate after having children. The typical woman joined a company in what is known as an 'administrative track' (*ippan shoku*

---

[31] *Nippon.com*, 22 June 2018: https://www.nippon.com/en/features/h00222/japanese-population-decline-accelerates-as-annual-births-fall-further-below-1-million.html.

[32] *Nikkei Asian Review*, 7 October 2019: https://asia.nikkei.com/Economy/Fertility-crash-Japan-s-births-headed-below-900-000-this-year.

[33] *Nippon.com*, 6 February 2019: https://www.nippon.com/en/in-depth/a06004/japan's-historic-immigration-reform-a-work-in-progress.html.

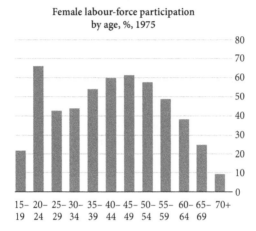

Female labour-force participation
by age, %, 1975

Figure 2.1 Female labour participation by age, 1975.
Source: Statistics Japan

in Japanese) role rather than a 'career-track' (*sogo shoku*) role, in the mutual knowledge that she would likely leave in her late 20s and early 30s. If she returned to work later in life it would be in an even lowlier, probably part-time, role. Figure 2.1 for 1975 and Figure 2.2 for 2015 show how this 'M' has flattened considerably in recent decades but does still exist—as it also does in most other advanced countries, at least to some extent.

The crucial question is not, however, whether women take time off to have children but rather what this does to their careers as and when they wish to return. In past decades, with most women firmly on the administrative track and firmly prepared to give up work for the sake of a family this did not much matter. It is still the case that more than 80 per cent of those classified as being on this administrative track are female.[34] But now, with more female university graduates having entered the workforce and having sought fully professional careers, whether through the *sogo shoku* track in big firms, by joining firms that do not use this two-track system, or by entering specialist functions such as the law or accountancy, it does matter.

The difficulty posed by this two-track system in big companies is its rigidity. It essentially requires applicants to make a choice on entering the firm which will be, to all intents and purposes,

---

[34] Goldman Sachs (2019), p. 25.

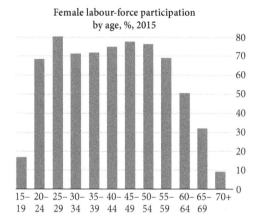

Female labour-force participation
by age, %, 2015

Figure 2.2 Female labour participation by age, 2015.
Source: Statistics Japan

irrevocable. This is now changing in some large companies in the face of changing preferences among staff. But also demographic realities make it no longer sensible to consign virtually an entire gender to a non-meritocratic future with little training or development.

Hitotsubashi University in Tokyo is the country's oldest and most prestigious commercial university—somewhat broader in scope than an American-style business school, but nevertheless the closest Japanese equivalent. Its female alumni have therefore been among the likeliest women to enter and hold on to career-track positions. In 2017–18 the university collaborated with a female alumni group known as 'Hitotsubashi Women Leaders for Innovation' (HWLI), or Hermes in its more popular name, in order to make a survey[35] of its alumni's career paths. The survey received 525 responses from Hitotsubashi graduates, of which 226 were male, 298 female, and the gender of one proved to be unknown. The highest proportion, for both males and females, were working in large companies. The respondents were of all ages, but especially well-represented between the ages of 30 and 59. Naturally, the share of female respondents was higher in the younger age groups as female admissions have

[35] Presentation to special roundtable at Hitotsubashi University for HWLI, 15 May 2018, *After Hitotsubashi University: Close look at the gender gap at work and at home, and the satisfaction*, by Asano Hiromi

risen in recent decades, but women still accounted for half the respondents even in the age cohort 50–59. More than 80 per cent of the male alumni were in full-time employment compared with about 73 per cent of the females. But although part-time employment was higher for the women than the men, it was still only around 5 per cent. Hitotsubashi alumni are clearly very different from the broader population.

What is especially interesting about this Hitotsubashi survey is what it tells us about the 'M' curve for better-qualified female alumni. While the survey was not able to map the whole working lives of its respondents to show how the 'M' had varied over time, its snapshot of who was in what sort of work now and at what age showed that although the respondents have a high employment rate at all ages compared with the norm, there is nevertheless a dip in that rate among alumni now aged in their 30s. The proportion in part-time work rises for older cohorts, especially in their 40s and 50s, though is still not high. In those age groups what does become more significant is self-employment, which rises to 20–25 per cent of respondents after the age of 30 or so. Most probably, this consists principally of women leaving careers in big companies to set up on their own as consultants. Among the male respondents, 63.8 per cent were in managerial positions at various levels, while this was true of only 33.4 per cent of the females. But a higher proportion of females than males were in specialized, non-managerial positions such as lawyers and accountants, which for some may be the precursor to moving later in life to self-employment.

This is a survey of an elite group. But although one cannot be sure, it might also be something of a pioneer group since now far more female students than in the past are studying in universities, among them quite a substantial number taking commercial or business administration courses of some kind. This is increasing the potential supply of female business leaders at all levels and in all regions. For example, from 2014–18 I was a visiting professor at a private university in Okayama, in western Japan, called Shujitsu, chiefly to give lectures in English once a year to their newly established business administration department. The students came mainly from Okayama Prefecture. In 2017 I interviewed[36] three female business administration students about their views on careers and family: their names are Itami Yuko, Kataoka Yuki, and Yamamura Yurika (who has a Nepalese mother and a Japanese father). Even ten, but certainly twenty years earlier, it would have been far harder to find female students such as these studying commerce in provincial universities.

Up to a point, they followed some of the typical patterns of Japanese female students. Itami-san and Kataoka-san had both been especially motivated to join Shujitsu by the fact that its business department is active in sending students to study abroad on exchange programmes as well as including mandatory internships at home and abroad. As Bando-san of Showa Women's University had pointed out in my earlier interview[37] with her, women need extra weapons if they are to battle their way through the male jungles of corporate Japan, and foreign experience and languages are two popular such weapons. I asked them about their career plans and all said they were looking for jobs in western Japan: one in branding or marketing, one perhaps the hotel business, the other the airline business.

What did they think about combining careers and family in the future, I asked? The answers were interestingly mixed, which suggested they were being quite frank and honest: one said she felt sure she could and would combine marriage and her career, and expected to use her maternity leave entitlement for that purpose; she said: 'I want the maternity system in companies to be improved, so that women can use it as a right rather than feeling guilty.' A second felt sure that if she had children she would want to give up work. The third (Yamamura-san, the Nepalese-Japanese) had more ambiguous views, saying she would definitely like to run a company eventually as its president and that she felt female students certainly had equal opportunities to those of male students, but that if she were to have children she would probably want to give up work at least for a while, perhaps returning a few years later. All, however,

---

[36] Interview on 7 July 2017, at Shujitsu University, Okayama.
[37] Interview with Bando Mariko on 6 December 2016, at Showa Women's University, Tokyo.

said that they wanted husbands' and wives' role in housework and child-rearing to be more equal than in the past.

Such views and such contradictory feelings about blending families and careers are typical the world over. They are simply coming later to Japan than they did to other advanced countries and only now is a sense of opportunity and possibility percolating widely among younger women. At least according to opinion polls, that sense of opportunity or of the barriers to it is not being accompanied by low levels of happiness or life satisfaction among Japanese women: as Professor Gill Steel of Doshisha University in Kyoto notes in her introduction to a recent edited volume,[38] despite the inequality and discrimination 'most studies show that Japanese women are happier than men and enjoy their lives more'. One reason that Steel posits for this is that 'despite these constraints, Japan is changing and a diversity of experience now exists among Japanese women that is not fully captured by conventional measures of gender equality'. In other words, women do have more choice and more freedom than in the past, enabling them to fulfil themselves in a myriad of ways. Being able to become president of Mitsubishi Corporation or prime minister of Japan are not the only tests of female empowerment. Part Two of this book will tell a similar story.

One female professional who has studied both men and women in work for nearly four decades is Fujiwara Mariko,[39] who herself rose to become director of the market-research wing of one of Japan's big advertising agencies, Hakuhodo Institute of Life and Living. She began to interview well-qualified women during the 1980s, especially those few who were graduating from top universities, and found that they tended to see themselves as 'special'. When companies did not treat them in a special manner[40] and instead had them making tea or doing routine tasks they would quit. In Fujiwara-san's view, they tended to give up too soon and still do: in her experience, the difference between women and men

[38] Gill Steel, *Introduction: Changing Women's and Men's Lives in Japan*, in 'Beyond the Gender Gap in Japan', ed. Gill Steel, Michigan Monograph Series in Japanese Studies 85 (2019).

[39] Interview with Fujiwara Mariko, 13 February 2018, Tokyo.

[40] For an illustration, see Kawai Eriko, ch. 9.

in Japan remains that women see working or a career as an option, not a responsibility, one they can always drop out from without stigma. Those who stay in companies are not very 'courageous in playing corporate games', she says. In particular, this means that unlike their male counterparts many women do not act as the generalists that are required for top management but instead become specialists. They do this for understandable reasons, namely to get more security. But it can mean that 'even after having worked for a long time, women get pigeon-holed and so do not get to the top'.

This raises a theme that is familiar to scholars of gender and work around the globe: the sense that women are less ambitious than men, or at least less confident about their prospects for advancement.[41] This shows up clearly in the Hitotsubashi survey too. Asked about their 'desire for career progression', the female alumni gave less ambitious or confident answers than the men in all age groups. Asked whether they were in jobs that were above their abilities, appropriate for them, or lower than their ability, there was a small but clear difference, with the men showing more confidence about their roles than the women. And, revealingly, more of the male respondents answered yes when asked whether in their careers they had been given particular experiences which may contribute to their confidence and ambition, such as 'participating in a cross-department project', 'starting up a new project or new business', or 'networking with external specialists'. Among these elite business alumni, the men are more confident at least in part because their careers have given them more of the tools they need for advancement.

That view from the Hitotsubashi alumni is reflected also in a study[42] for the Japan Institute for Labor Policy and Training (an affiliate of the Ministry of Health, Labour, and Welfare) in 2018. The researcher, Takami Tomohiro, found that even among male and female workers who had entered companies on the career-track (*sogo shoku*) there was clear evidence of gender segregation in terms

---

[41] See for example Anna Fels, *Do Women Lack Ambition?*, *Harvard Business Review*, April 2004.

[42] *Gender Segregation at Work in Japanese Companies: Focusing on Gender Disparities in Desire for Promotion*, *Japan Labor Issues* 2.11 (December 2018), Japan Institute for Labor Policy and Training.

of the tasks and experiences they are given to equip them for future advancement. As he wrote, 'It is evident that women are given relatively less experience with core duties that can lead to managerial positions'. An important contributor to this process is the availability to do regular overtime, Tamaki continued:

> In a corporate culture where long working hours are the standard or norm, women often must work overtime in order to handle the company's core duties. Japan in general has just such a corporate culture, meaning it is not easy for many female employees to utilize their full potential.

Of course, everywhere men or women who wish to rise to senior positions have to put in long hours and hard work when necessary. The point being made, however, is that in Japanese organizations it has not just been a matter of working hard. In an organizational culture in which belonging to the team is crucial, and in which in the past 'the team' consisted essentially of men, a central part of team-building has been working late together in the office and going out drinking together, often several times a week. Office workers—*salarymen* by the popular moniker—have been expected to show if anything more commitment to their companies than to their families in all respects except the financial. It remains to be seen whether the sudden need, thanks to the 2020 covid-19 pandemic for many companies to embrace remote working from home will endure, but if it does it has the potential to alter this team-based culture of commitment and 'presenteeism' in a way that could help the cause of working women quite markedly.

In countries in which there has been greater labour mobility between companies and in which as a result employment has a more transactional flavour, efforts at team-building are just as important but tend to be done in different ways, such as through bonding retreats, training courses, and the provision of collective amenities such as corporate cafeterias or sporting activities so as to bring people together. At Japanese firms, where employment is considered a long-term mutual commitment, but job rotation is quite routine, team-building has become a more constant process. And as it involves a lot of overtime and evening drinking with colleagues it is a very male process too, which has been hard for women with families to play a full part in. It is not coincidental that the sort of work—what Tamaki-san called 'core duties'—that leads to managerial promotion is allocated to the sort of employees believed to be able to do plenty of overtime and so good team players. In other words, men.

∗   ∗   ∗

To worry about whether Japanese women have the ambition or confidence to do well in their careers, if they choose to seek a career, may be interesting and ultimately important, but it is to jump a few steps ahead of where the country stands now. Given the currently low share of leadership positions held by women, the prior question to ask is whether Japanese women's current levels of ambition and confidence are being reflected in their career progress, and if not why not. For there is already a clear gap between existing ability, ambition, and progress, even before wondering about whether and how Japanese women might be made more ambitious and confident tomorrow.

A corporate culture in which being part of the team by sharing long working hours is prized above virtually all else forms a central part of the problem for women—at least for those women who want to also have families. Leaving such teams even for maternity leave still feels like letting the team down, just as paternity leave does for fathers. Yet although this group culture is particularly intense in Japanese companies, this syndrome would not really come as a surprise to working mothers (or, more recently, fathers) in companies in Europe or North America. The presidential candidacy of the billionaire businessman Michael Bloomberg was dogged in its early days by old allegations that he had shown sexist attitudes as an employer, including over female employees getting pregnant.[43] The real point is that organizations of all kinds need to build planning for absences for maternity and paternity leave into their budgeting, staffing, and project management, so that absences do not 'let the team down'. After all, the long human gestation cycle at least gives plenty of notice. That is what European and American organizations have

---

[43] See Megan Garber, *The Atlantic*, 19 September 2018: https://www.theatlantic.com/entertainment/archive/2018/09/mike-bloomberg-comments-women-metoo/570448/; or Mairead McArdle, *National Review*, 14 November 2019: https://www.nationalreview.com/news/bloomberg-responded-kill-it-after-employee-disclosed-her-pregnancy-1997-lawsuit-alleges/.

had to learn to do during the past few decades, generally from a pretty un-family-friendly starting point.

A landmark law introduced by the Abe government and passed by the Diet in June 2018 has tried to help solve part of this problem, although it was not explicitly aimed at improving gender equality as such. This was the Work-Style Reform Bill,[44] whose measures came into effect from April 2019. This omnibus law aimed to deal with several different issues, but its two main targets were excessive working hours and the unequal treatment of workers on regular and non-regular contracts concerning pay and conditions. Prime Minister Abe said in a statement after the law had passed that:

> These are the first major reforms [to labour laws] in 70 years. We will rectify the problems of working long hours, and eradicate the expression 'non-regular employment' from Japan.[45]

One prediction can be made with some certainty: this reform will not succeed in eradicating the phrase 'non-regular employment' from Japanese discourse. That is because although legislating for equal pay for equal work, whether it is by full-time, part-time, or fixed-term contract workers, is welcome it cannot deal with two salient points about non-regular work. These are that non-regular workers are often used by companies for different tasks from those performed by regular workers, so that inequality of pay is not always pertinent; and that it is the insecurity of non-regular work that makes it distinct, a characteristic that leads both employer and employee to avoid investing time and money in training and skill development in the knowledge that such effort may well be wasted.

The problems of working long hours could well, however, be mitigated by this legislation as long as it is properly enforced, a mitigation which could help male and female workers alike to become more productive and to devote more time to their families. The law put a limit on overtime of 45 hours per month and 360 hours per year, except in 'temporary, special circumstances', but

---

[44] *Japan Labor Issues* 2.10, November 2018.   [45] Ibid.

with restrictions placed on any such 'temporary' agreements too. There is also an exemption for 'specialist professions', which are allowed to pay by performance rather than work hours. It is all quite complicated and will in the end depend on enforcement and interpretation. The effort to reduce working hours might seem paradoxical for a country facing a labour shortage, but the issue of *karoshi* or death by overwork has been a major public concern for several decades now.

During the first decade of this century, recorded deaths from *karoshi* were totalling 150–160 per year, but numbers have thankfully declined to 80–100 annually in the past five years, though all these numbers may be understated as some suicides may not be fully attributable to a particular cause.[46] A particularly notorious case was the 2015 suicide by a 24-year-old female employee of Dentsu, the country's top advertising agency, after having put in 105 hours of overtime in a month.[47] Dentsu was subsequently fined a mere Y500,000 for making workers do overtime beyond the then laxer legal limits.[48]

At the time of writing, it is too soon to assess how much influence the Work-Style Reform Bill will have on the culture of long working hours and of unpaid and 'social' overtime. It is unlikely to change working habits quickly, but it could apply a gradual squeeze on the practice and help encourage companies to think of new ways to operate. One of the main reasons why progress is slow is that decision-makers in corporate and other organizations about working styles and human resources practices are generally men in their 40s, 50s, or even 60s. The slow ascent of women into management means that in most companies there is not yet a critical mass of female managers making or being involved in such decisions. But, as Bando-san of Showa Women's University said,[49] the much larger pipeline of female graduates seeking careers means that the number

---

[46] Takami Tomohiro, *Current State of Working Hours and Overwork in Japan*, Japan Labor *Issues* 3.19 (November 2019).

[47] *Japan Times*, 14 July 2017: https://www.japantimes.co.jp/opinion/2017/07/14/editorials/dentsu-karoshi-case-goes-trial/#.Xgic4C2cbf8.

[48] *Reuters*, 6 October 2017.

[49] Interview with Bando Mariko, at Showa Women's University, Tokyo, 6 December 2016.

of female section chiefs, divisional managers, and senior managers is likely to double during the coming decade, reaching 25 per cent or more. That, in combination with efforts such as those of the 30 per cent Club to boost female representation on boards, is likely to create that sort of critical mass between now and 2030.

As well as that critical mass being important for its influence on decision-making in companies, universities, ministries, local government, the police, and other sorts of organizations, it is also important for creating and providing role models for younger women to learn from and in some cases to seek to emulate. In past decades, although there were always some successful women in all sorts of spheres, they were such rare exceptions that they were likelier to confirm to younger generations how difficult it would be to become a successful scientist, novelist, diplomat, entrepreneur, academic, bureaucrat, or manager, not how feasible it was. In Britain too, it is not at all clear that Margaret Thatcher's defeat of all the societal odds in the 1950s, 60s, and 70s to become the country's first female prime minister really acted to inspire or reassure younger women, although she may have helped prove to the many misogynist doubters that a women was perfectly capable of political leadership and even statecraft.

Now, even though women still occupy fairly few leadership roles in Japan, there is a much larger supply of female success stories in all sorts of fields, grand or humble. Today's much more numerous role models, of women of all ages who have made great achievements in their chosen occupations, also mean that, bit by bit, old clichés and stereotypes about what women can or cannot do—such as whether women are capable of managing teams, of making decisions, of starting and building enterprises, of pursuing successful scientific research—are being challenged in Japan, just as they have been in other advanced countries. Those clichés and stereotypes have persisted for longer in Japan than elsewhere, partly because of the lack of role models and associated evidence to prove the contrary. Part Two will now look at some of that evidence by means of interviews with twenty-one Japanese women who have been notably successful, organized into themes.

PART TWO
SUCCESS STORIES

3
Individuals with a Community Spirit

Baba Kanako, Ishizaka Noriko, and Oikawa Hideko

'From when I was young, I always felt I had something different from the others. I was always independent and not in the group.' That comment by Baba Kanako,[1] who runs a school-uniform recycling business in Takamatsu City, on Shikoku island in the south-western part of the Japanese archipelago, encapsulates one of the central dilemmas in thinking about the future role of women in Japan. If women are to succeed in making their own choices, in swimming against the powerful currents of convention and of male prejudice, they will often need to have quite an independent spirit. Often, they will be the sort of person who does things differently from others, not one who follows a typical, well-worn track. Yet if we are to expect such spirits to have an impact on Japan rather than just on their own lives, even to help shape the future of the country, then they also need to be part of or connected to whatever is their 'group', for Japan is a strongly communitarian society. To change Japan must be to change the group, at all levels of society.

That is why it was instructive and inspiring to find and meet three quite independent spirits who have nevertheless focused their minds and their work on making a social contribution, on supporting and improving their respective communities, rather than only making profits or other individualistic goals. They are swimming against the currents, but in a socially positive, community-oriented way.

---

[1] Interview with Baba Kanako at Sakuraya, Takamatsu City, Shikoku, 12 July 2017.

The first two of these women share one word—recycling—but are otherwise quite different from one another. Ishizaka Noriko rose, at the early age of just 30, to become president of her father's waste-recycling company, Ishizaka Sangyo, in Saitama prefecture about an hour outside Tokyo, with a mission and ambition to change the rather negative image the company had gained in its own neighbourhood. She is an independent, determined spirit working within a family company, seeking to recuperate her business's environmental reputation within the local community and to build a sense of mutual involvement between the community and the company.

The other, the aforementioned Baba Kanako, is a single mother of three children living in Takamatsu City who found she could not afford new school uniforms for her kids and decided, against much advice from male business executives, to set up a shop dedicated to buying and reselling used uniforms, which remarkably was the first of its kind in Japan. That shop, called Sakuraya, now involves volunteers and staff from the local community and inspired Baba-san to set up a company, Sunglad, offering advice to mothers' groups all over Japan about how to develop similar social enterprises recycling school uniforms.

In their different ways, both women are challenging traditional assumptions, both about Japan and about women. Ishizaka-san is challenging the idea that waste-disposal and recycling are dirty, dangerous, very masculine businesses suitable only for male employees. It is no coincidence that when I left the Ishizaka Sangyo offices after our interview,[2] I was handed as a gift two 'pound cakes' made with materials grown and produced on a farm on the land surrounding the waste-recycling facility.

Nor, I suspect, is it a coincidence that the very business-like Ishizaka-san wears the longest fingernails I have ever seen on a chief executive, whether female or male. (On the day I visited, they were painted a bright white colour.) Her business is about dealing with materials from the construction industry, but that does not make it simply manual work. Recycling, in Ishizaka-san's view,

---

[2] Interview with Ishizaka Noriko, Ishizaka Sangyo Head Office, Miyoshi-machi, Saitama Prefecture, 27 November 2017.

should be about making the environment cleaner and more natural, not a dirty affair dedicated to creating dust and pollution. Nor should this business simply be one run by men: half of Ishizaka Sangyo's managers are females. I imagine she uses her fingernails as symbols to emphasize these points.

Down on Shikoku, Baba-san is challenging the idea that second-hand clothes for children are somehow shameful and un-Japanese. When she researched the potential market, she found that the only company in the whole country re-selling school uniforms was one in Tokyo that was doing so for the sex trade. Now there are more than thirty enterprises all around Japan emulating what Sakuraya has done. The two firms that dominate the market for new school uniforms are beginning to get worried about this competition. And, equally remarkably, with both her businesses Baba-san managed to make her working hours fit well with spending time with her three children, who are now (in 2020) aged 22, 20, and 15, but were all nine years younger than that when she started Sakuraya in 2011. She has shown that running a business can give a woman more control over her time, not less, when compared with working for somebody else's company or organization and being told what to do.

The third of these individualistic women, Oikawa Hideko,[3] is quite different. She showed her determination as well as business talent when she took over the stewardship of her family textiles business when her husband suddenly died and has made a success of it in a tough competitive environment. But it was the dramatic and tragic 2011 tsunami off the eastern coast of Japan's main island, Honshu, with the worst damage and death toll in the northern region where Oikawa-san lives and works, that thrust her and her company to the centre of the local community when her factory and warehouse became, essentially, an evacuation camp.

* * *

Baba-san is unusual in other ways too. When I first read about the fact that she is a single mother of three kids, and that she had been

[3] Interview with Oikawa Hideko, Oikawa Denim, Kesennuma, Miyagi Prefecture, 30 November 2016.

unable to afford new uniforms, I immediately assumed she must be divorced. The number of single parents is small in Japan although it has grown in recent years, but as very few children are born outside marriage it is almost invariably associated with divorce. This is true in Baba-san's case too, except for the fact that only two of the three children came from her seven-year-long marriage; the third came from a later partnership with another man, from whom she has also now separated. In both cases for a time she gave up work and became a full-time mother and housewife. But as she told me, she 'could not accept the confinement of the household and liked instead to go out'. She says she is 'not always good at communicating with others', which she thinks may explain why she split up from the two men. 'Usually,' she said, 'Japanese husbands try to bind their wives to home, like birds in a cage.' But she says she is too independent to accept that.

Aware that this is far from typical in Japan, I asked her whether this unusual and somewhat rebellious nature gave her problems with the other mothers who buy school uniforms at Sakuraya or work with her. After all, they will be more conventional wives and mothers than her, especially in a small provincial city such as Takamatsu, and there is often said to be a stigma related to single motherhood. Her answer was that her status as a single mother of three caused no problems with the other mothers. She feels others respected her for working on her own to support a family, noticing the fact that she also found plenty of time to spend with her children. A crucial part of this building of trust and respect came when she decided to open a shop rather than distributing uniforms from her home: at that point what she was doing became more visible, presented for all to see in a clean and smart way, and gradually more and more local people became involved. The social enterprise became part of the local community.

From my visit to Sakuraya in Takamatsu, I was left in no doubt that Baba-san is quite an unusual person. She even came to the airport to meet me and my assistant and drove us personally to her shop. Talking about her own childhood and schooldays, she told me that she had been quite competitive in physical education classes and in sport, specializing in sports based on strength such as shot put and throwing the discus, and winning competitions. For that reason, she studied at Tokyo Women's College of Physical Education. She did regular physical training for ten years, including the bench press and weight training, and says that it taught her about endurance.

Most particularly, she says that the experience forced her to think a lot about why she was doing the training, and the relationship between how she was training and how she was competing. I asked her whether she still does physical training now. Her answer was that she does two hundred sit-ups every day and consumes protein drinks. My impression is that she considers this as a rather light exercise regime, but it sounded quite tough to me and Baba-san does look strong and energetic.

Certainly, she showed determination as well as thoughtfulness when she was setting up her business. After graduating from college, she worked for the Shikoku branch of the Nichido Fire and Marine Insurance company (now part of Tokyo Marine and Fire) in the sales force for four years until she got married and quit her job. Then when she got divorced the only employment she could initially get that fit in with raising her children was distributing flyers for a pizza restaurant, usually while wheeling her baby in a stroller. What she really wanted to do, she says, was to start a business that could allow her to control her time sufficiently to be able to be with her kids when they needed her. Her first daughter, in fact, is disabled and needed both a special school and special attention. The idea for a business selling second-hand school uniforms came when she faced the need to buy new uniforms for her second daughter in the fourth grade at elementary school and again in fifth grade and realized she couldn't really afford to pay (for example) Y14,000 just for a new 'sailor' top each year, plus all the other parts of the uniform as well as a smart school back-pack, even though by then she had returned to work in sales for an insurance firm.

Baba-san worked out, she says, that she needed savings of about Y3 million to be able to start her business. Her work at the insurance company meant that she could start saving up in a small way, and meanwhile she consulted local executives at the firm about her business idea. All of them raised objections, saying that no Japanese mothers would want second-hand uniforms and that such a firm would not survive as a business. But she felt sure there must be untapped demand from mothers who were similarly poor, and also saw that some second-hand businesses in other goods were starting to get established in Japan. Times were changing. Despite finding that there was not a single shop in the whole of Japan doing what she planned to do, she decided to go ahead and give it a try.

At first, she tried to run the business from home, distributing adverts through letter boxes just as she had with pizza flyers, and doing the washing and other preparation of uniforms herself while writing an online blog to publicize it. But that way she found she couldn't get other mothers either to trust her or really to understand what it was she was trying to do, which was why she decided she had to spend more money and open a shop. This was in early 2011, by when she had accumulated a stock of fifty uniforms. With the stock thus on display, news about the idea spread in Takamatsu, and women started to come to the shop to take a look.

Although she bargained down the rent with the landlord by arguing that helping mothers was a worthwhile thing to do, she still had too little cash to really get the enterprise going. Borrowing money from banks proved very hard both as a single mother and because she was doing a new and untested type of business. But then she had what proved to be a very bright and successful idea: she spotted a competition being run by Kagawa Prefecture (of which Takamatsu is the capital) offering a Y3 million prize for the most promising new businesses.

At first, the competition's process felt rather like she was just repeating her discouraging consultations with male life insurance executives. For the prize, she had to be interviewed by committees of elderly men who said sceptical things about her business and its prospects. I suspect she fought back, hard. She says she told them she was sure that as more mothers were now working, society was changing. Mothers often have too little contact with their neighbours and local community to be able to get the help they need, and so she was sure there must be demand for the sort of help her business was offering. To her surprise, she got through to the final stage, as one of a short-list of six businesses, and had to give a public presentation in front of a big audience. The main point in her presentation was her idea and ambition of spreading her business to the whole of Japan, for she argued that there were similar needs everywhere. And so she won the prize, and spent the Y3 million on a point-of-sale cash register system to professionalize the business.

The main lesson of this success was not just the cash, however: it was the value of the free publicity that winning the prize brought. She started to enter other prize competitions, and won again. This had the further benefit of attracting attention in the media, with the result that Tokyo Broadcasting System[4] filmed an interview with her in 2015 as part of a series introducing interesting new businesses. This sparked off enquiries and visitors from all over Japan.

That brought a lot of fresh inquiries to Baba-san's second business, the consulting or advisory business to help other uniform-recycling social enterprises elsewhere in Japan. She had set up this business under the name of Sunglad in 2013, two years after opening her Sakuraya shop. She didn't have time to train people from all over the country about how to set up a school-uniform business, so she didn't want to establish a franchise business (like McDonalds restaurants do). Instead, she provides advice on how to set up and run a business like hers, for an initial once-off contract fee of Y1.7 million and then a monthly payment. Clients pay Sunglad fees ranging between Y3,500 and Y6,500 a month, depending (among other things) on whether the business wishes to become associated with Baba-san's now popular blog. The result of all this is that while Sakuraya's sales turnover in its first year was just Y1.2 million, the combined annual sales of Sakuraya/Sunglad have now reached Y35 million. Baba-san is the sole owner of Sunglad and the firm pays her a salary.

There are two crucial elements to the success of these businesses, beyond Baba-san's energy and determination. One has been the involvement of the Takamatsu community. Realizing she needed her school uniforms to be cleaned and knowing the task was getting too big for her alone, Baba-san had the idea of offering the job to a

---

[4] Tokyo Broadcasting System is a national TV and radio network affiliated with the Mainichi daily newspaper.

facility for the disabled that her elder daughter had attended and which was short of work and money. Initially, too, she did the job of removing embroidered names and labels from the uniforms herself, which took about thirty minutes for each tag. One day an elderly woman visited her shop, saw what was needed, and offered to help. Now all of that sewing, for what is now a stock of 14,000 uniforms, is done by local women for a bit of extra cash.

The second vital element, alongside this social contribution, has been to limit the opening hours of the shop to 10.00am to 15.00pm so that Baba-san and the mothers that work there have time to devote to their children when they come home from school. This probably reduces overall sales, but the clear purpose of the business is anyway social contribution rather than profit, by making motherhood easier and more economical in a collaborative way. The shop opens on Saturdays so that working mothers have a chance to visit then, and she opens by special appointment, too.

I asked Baba-san what mistakes she had made while getting the business going. She answered, with a wry smile, that the first difficulty she had to grapple with was to avoid selling uniforms to the sex trade. The second, however, was tougher: it was to work out how to price uniforms, whether as a purchaser or a seller. She says it took three years to work this out, as there are so many hundreds of schools and as there were no existing businesses doing the same thing. This is one of the most valuable pieces of information that Sunglad is able to supply to the increasing numbers of businesses all around Japan that are trying to do the same thing. As the number of those other shops increases, she is also able to collect data from more and more of them in return for her advice.

There are now about forty businesses all over Japan that have been advised by Baba-san and Sunglad. Soon, she is thinking of setting up an office in Tokyo so that she can speak to visitors and potential clients from the eastern side of Japan. I asked her how big the market could become. Her answer was that the maximum number of such shops in Japan was probably about one hundred. Her aim is to become head of a nationwide mothers' organization, gaining data and selling it. Certainly, the growth of these second-hand school uniforms businesses is beginning to create concern at the three dominant, one might even say oligopolistic, manufacturers of new school uniforms, which she claims do things like threaten seamstresses to persuade them not to work for the second-hand sellers. If competition from enterprises such as Sakuraya makes those firms lower their prices, that would surely be a good thing for families everywhere.

Baba-san can have the final word. She says that 'I want this way of doing business to be infectious.' What she means by that is that she wants to encourage other women to form types of businesses that involve the locality, with elderly women working in the shop as volunteers, for example, and offering work such as cleaning to local schools for disabled children. 'When I start training mothers [on how to set up a uniforms business], I call it a community business, even though you can also get some profit. In Japan, it is very import-ant to keep the community.'

*   *   *

Ishizaka-san would certainly agree, even though her family's business is of a more conventional, profit-making sort. She is also different from Baba-san in neither being an entrepreneur in her own right, nor a single mother: she has taken over leadership of her father's business, and she is married with two university-age children. Her son is majoring in economics and her daughter is studying management and ecology at a university in the United States. She says that both are anxious eventually to work for the family com-pany, just as their mother did, joining in 1992 at the age of 20. So far, so conventional.

What is different and striking about Ishizaka-san's story is that she decided she wanted to take over as president of her father's company, at the young age of just 30, only ten years after joining the firm. After a long period of discussion he chose to allow her to, though he did not hand over his full authority in the company to her for a further eleven years, which happened in 2013 when she was 41. By then, she had transformed the firm and proved herself an innovator in what is a conservative, somewhat old-fashioned industry.

How? Well, the answer begins with what motivated her to push to become president at such a young age. The trigger was a growing controversy in the media and in her firm's neighbourhood in Saitama prefecture about pollution being caused by her industry, and locally in their town of Miyoshi-machi by Ishizaka Sangyo in particular. When I visited the company, I could see straight away what is distinctive about this industry, especially in a very densely populated country like Japan, in which farming takes place in smallholdings even in quite urban areas. As it is costly to transport waste materials from houses and factories that are demolished, the materials tend to be processed locally, in populated areas. Building materials contain a lot of substances that, when the products are broken up, can be toxic or bad for health. Older buildings, constructed in the 1950s or 1960s when controls on materials were more lax or else scientific knowledge of toxicity was less than today, are particularly likely to release such toxins if proper care is not exercised when the demolished materials are being processed.

The recycling or processing industry is therefore both essential and problematic. What Ishizaka-san says woke her up to the problems was a series of news reports about dioxins from waste materials contaminating vegetables, produced by the sort of incinerators being used in her industry. Ishizaka Sangyo was the target of lawsuits alleging involvement in such pollution, which she says was unfair as their company's incinerators were already a newer and cleaner sort but nevertheless local trust had been broken. Pressure grew to force the firm out of business or to make it move elsewhere.

What Ishizaka-san sought to do in response is to clean up her company as well as its image, and turn it into a premium quality, higher technology company in this old-fashioned sector. That transformation has also been reflected in Ishizaka Sangyo's business model: their fees are now nearly 1.5 times as high as the industry average, and, Ishizaka-san told me, 'we hope to charge twice the industry average' eventually. To charge higher fees requires the firm to offer a superior service, which they have sought to do by using better technology to increase the proportion of the materials they receive that are recycled, which thereby reduces the quantity that have to go into landfill or that risk penalties to the customer for unlawful dumping. Suppliers of waste who sort it themselves into more categories, making it easier to recycle, can pay lower fees. In effect, Ishizaka Sangyo has changed from being an incinerator of waste to a reclamation company. The firm now says it is able to process 98 per cent of the materials it receives.

What is vital for the company's reputation locally is its new openness and its ecological investments. Unlike many of its competitors, Ishizaka-san told me, her firm has become able to ensure that all its equipment is kept inside the buildings, preventing dust and other pollution from leaking out, and it washes the tyres and bodywork of all vehicles going in and out, for the same reason. Beyond that, she has invited neighbouring residents to come inside the factory too, both for ordinary visits and as school groups. She says the firm receives five thousand schoolchildren every year, and she tries to teach them about why the environment needs to be protected. Her aim, she said, 'is to teach them why processing of materials is costly and why users must bear the cost', but also why there is a 'need to produce goods with future waste in mind', in other words with reduced packaging and with materials that can more easily be processed and recycled.

This emphasis on education has also been extended to employees. Ishizaka-san told me that when she joined the company more than twenty-five years ago, she 'was shocked to see that the average salary was lower than in manufacturing firms'. Since taking over as president, she has worked to upgrade the level of training and skills of employees, and in the past five years has raised the base salary by 15 per cent, which means that it is now nearing the level of manufacturers. This has been done while changing the workforce by attrition so that the average age has fallen from 55 to 35, as many older workers chose to leave. The purpose of the internal education has been so that 'employees see how they contribute to society' even while they are doing work that is demanding, dirty, and sometimes dangerous. Employees have been required to attend one study session each month, geared towards obtaining an ISO standard for environmental management.

The investment Ishizaka-san has made in the natural environment within which her factory sits is important for its contribution to, and relations with, the community. About 80 per cent of the company's land consists of a park and farms, and only 20 per cent is accounted for by the factory. Hence the pound-cakes I was handed as I left.

Ishizaka-san has clearly thought a lot about women's contribution in companies and management, as well as about her business and the environment. Only 30 per cent of the firm's employees are women, but half of the management. I asked her what impression she has about the attitude to women in her industry, and in her own company. She answered by first pointing out that her waste-processing industry of course has its own industry association, with chapters for each prefecture, but that at the moment among the heads and deputy heads of the prefectural associations there is not even one woman. In the Saitama prefectural association, Ishizaka-san is the only female.

She believes that mindsets have to change, both for men and for women. 'I believe that a company that cannot use women effectively cannot survive.' She said that 'the male mindset is strong and unchanging.' I asked her to define the male mindset. Her answer: 'not being willing to listen to women's opinions; thinking that women are good only for serving tea and sake.' She felt quite a lot had changed in the Tokyo area in recent years, but not in other parts of the country. But she also said that women need to change their mindsets too. 'They should be more active in taking over management and offering their visions about strategy.'

*   *   *

My third individual with a community spirit has shown a strong vision about strategy. While not exactly in the recycling business, unlike the other two, she has in a real sense recycled her entire company. She succeeded in turning the business around and recovering from severe setbacks on several occasions, beginning with the death of her husband. But the biggest setback of all was a community one, one to which Oikawa Hideko and her company chose to respond in a generous and important community way. This was the devastation wrought to the Kesennuma area in Tohoku by what is now known as the Great East Japan Earthquake and tsunami on 11 March 2011 or, in a nod to New York's '9/11' terrorist atrocity in 2001, '3/11'.

Just before 3/11, things had been going well for the company, which is called Oikawa Denim. They had chosen to consolidate two factories into one site, gaining efficiency and reducing costs. In February a call had come to Oikawa-san from the British Embassy in Tokyo, conveying a request from a clothing maker in Manchester who was looking for 'the best denim maker in Japan'. But then just two weeks after that very flattering call came the disaster. The waters of the tsunami fortunately did not quite reach the factory, which is on high ground looking out over the bay, but the company's warehouse was washed away, containing a stock of around six thousand pairs of jeans. More important, staff and neighbours lost homes and offices, and the factory instantly became an impromptu evacuation centre for 150 people, including a twenty-day-old baby.

There was no electricity, and lighting had to be just by candles. Luckily one delivery vehicle that was stranded nearby turned out to be full of supplies it had been taking to a convenience store, and contained a stock of drinks destined for vending machines as well as milk for the baby. Oikawa-san says that everyone huddled together. 'For three days people couldn't raise their faces, as they had lost everything.' On the third day, Oikawa-san's managerial instincts kicked in, as she looked for ways to cheer people up. 'I set up an organization for people, giving out roles and titles, such as head of cooking, getting people to sort out tasks such as clearing rubble from the road. There were no complaints. In fact it was like living in the old way, collecting firewood and co-operating with one another.'

In the mud and rubble, they later found about forty to fifty pairs of the jeans that had been washed away from the warehouse and brought them back. 'Looking at the jeans made me cry,' she said, 'as I saw them as survivors. There was no damage to the stitching or the materials.' This was soon broadcast as a story by a visiting NHK reporter, Doden Aiko, who described these 'survivors' as 'miracle jeans'. But also that visit by Doden-san restored the evacuees' sense of being connected to the outside world. On 4 April, Oikawa Denim was able to restart production using generators to power the sewing machines. They had no mains electricity until the end of May, and water supplies were reconnected only at the beginning of June. Only on 24 July did the evacuees leave the factory to move to temporary housing. Overall, half of Oikawa Denim's employees lost their houses and Oikawa-san was still living in a temporary home when I visited her in November 2016, nearly six years after the disaster.

'For me, the recovery from the tsunami meant the ability to stand on our own feet,' Oikawa-san told me. In fact, the whole history of Oikawa Denim is one of recovery from difficulties, what an American might call a roller-coaster ride.

She and her husband had started the business in 1981, converting an old family company run by her husband's parents that had made traditional kimonos. (Oikawa-san had moved from Niigata on the west coast of Japan's main island to Tohoku on the east coast to marry him.) The kimono business had been in decline and a whole-saler asked the firm whether it might be interested in making denim instead to supply jeans to be sold by other companies. Oikawa-san at that time was teaching abacus to children in a local school. She and her husband thought it was a good opportunity, and there were local seamstresses they could hire and train to sew the jeans. Oikawa-san took charge of the accounts and the administration. She realized, she says, that 'the accounts were the core of the business.'

Things went well. But then ten years later came the sudden death of her husband. They had three young sons. One option was to return home to her own family in Niigata who would have helped to look after the children. But the business had a good order-book so Oikawa-san decided to take over as president and run the firm herself. Soon after she took over, a local government grant enabled her local town to send a delegation of twelve women on a visit to the United States, which was very unusual at the time. The nearly two weeks she spent there, in Ohio with a homestay and then in New York City, were evidently quite inspirational for her, especially in terms of giving her a glimpse of global markets and global standards.

This helped when the next setback came, at the end of the 1990s. As Japan's economic growth stagnated in this post-bubble period, domestic demand for jeans slumped at the same time as cheap competition from other Asian producers was on the rise. The contracts from big jeans labels such as Wrangler and Edwin started to be lost to overseas suppliers.

Oikawa-san's response was that in order to survive the company really needed to design and make its own products, moving upmarket to establish itself as a premium, luxury brand both in its own right and as a supplier to other luxury labels. 'I said to my sons and to employees that they should try to design and make a product that they really want to wear themselves.' It was a long process of trial and error, including having their employees learn how to sell the jeans directly themselves rather than through big wholesalers. Adjustment in this way was costly as well as time-consuming, but Oikawa-san came up with a smart idea to keep the firm going while they were developing these new products: 'I thought of what domestic Japanese sewing markets might exist, and thought of the Self-Defence Forces and the police, whose uniforms would be bought at home for reasons of confidentiality or security of supply.' Fortunately, in 2001–2 when the SDF sent its staff to contribute to the US-led reconstruction efforts in Afghanistan, a lot of uniforms were needed, and Oikawa was taken on as a subcontractor.

Supported by that contract, Oikawa Denim proceeded to set up their own brand of jeans, Studio Zero, using special techniques and strong linen thread—which in turn needed a new machine to sew it. Oikawa-san's third son, who is an engineer, developed that new machine, which she says was the first time in the world that linen thread had been able to be used with denim, a fact that drew some TV coverage. Now about 20 per cent of Oikawa Denim's production is for its own brands, and 80 per cent goes to other labels, all of which are themselves premium brands. From sales of their newest brand, Shiro, a percentage is donated to help with disaster relief.

Oikawa Denim is not a big company—it has just twenty-two employees, and simply one factory—but its chance of surviving and thriving through the next generation will depend on its ability to continue to develop its products as top quality, luxury items. The foundation for that has been laid over the past quarter of a century by the leadership and determination of Oikawa Hideko, the woman who used to teach abacus in schools. In November 2017 she handed over the presidency of the firm to her son, Hiroshi, passing on to the next generation, although she is still there as a guide and inspiration. Hers has been a career-long exercise in leadership.

4

Leadership in a Male World

Kono Naho, Higuchi Hiroe, and Terada Chiyono

In Britain in the early days when women were starting to rise through the ranks of what had been conventionally male organizations the stories told in objection to this trend were pretty much the same as those that can be heard in Japan today. Some men said that women were 'too emotional' to take on management responsibilities, which required rationality and logic of the sort associated by the speakers with men, of course. Others claimed women innately lacked the ability to command respect or convey authority, especially among a mainly male staff—making the problem a circular one, in which women could not rise because the staff were mainly male, and the staff were mainly male because women could not rise. Sometimes the prospect of women managing teams of men was dealt with through male jokes involving sexual innuendo so as to undermine the idea and the person's image. Depressingly often— and in my work in Italy I have heard this all the time—the promotion of a woman was greeted with whispered accusations that she must have used her looks or even actual sexual favours to achieve her success. There could be no other explanation. Sexual harassment of female subordinates or even equals was widespread. Men, it seemed, found it difficult to accept being given orders by women or even working alongside them. Perhaps they felt in some sense intimidated or psychologically emasculated by the idea. Nothing is new or unique about the male prejudice and fears that are heard in Japan today.

Such accusations are still heard from British males, but less frequently than in the past. The idea of women managing men is not unusual or controversial any more. But it is not yet so 'normal' to have women in leadership positions, managing mixed teams of men and women, that nobody notices the sex of a chief executive or senior manager. It is still noteworthy, especially in big industrial companies, for a woman to become chief executive or chief financial officer. Hopefully the day will come when it just feels normal, but that still seems a long way ahead. That situation is clearly even further away in Japan, where male prejudices and fears remain dominant. But as in Britain during the 1970s, 1980s, and 1990s, a generation of role models among female leaders is showing that women certainly can exercise leadership successfully in organizations that are full of men. The ways in which they do so vary as much among women managers as they do between men and women, or indeed as much as leadership methods vary among men.

Kono Naho was, at first glance when I interviewed[1] her, a typically smiling, smartly dressed young Japanese woman. Her achievements and her responsibilities make her far from typical, however, and she is clearly tough and determined. She is president of Rakuten Ichiba, the e-commerce division of Rakuten and thus Japan's largest e-commerce company. As a result, she is the most senior female executive at Rakuten—in fact, she is the only woman at the top executive officer level in the Rakuten group. (Since I interviewed her, she has added the title of Chief Marketing Officer for the whole group to her roles.) Her division employs 3,500 people, or 25 per cent of the whole group's staff, and she has sixteen people reporting directly to her. Only one of those sixteen is a woman. Being the digital, entrepreneurial, very twenty-first-century company that it is, Rakuten's staff are generally younger than at a traditional Japanese firm. Even so, aged in her early 40s, Kono-san is unusually young for a top executive officer. Some of her direct reports are quite a bit older than her.

To have older people working for you is not so unusual in British firms, especially in services businesses. When I became chief editor of *The Economist* in 1993, I was only 36 years old. Probably

---

[1] Interview with Kono Naho, Rakuten Head Office, Crimson House, Futakotamagawa, Tokyo, 26 October 2016.

somewhere between one-third and one-half of my journalists were older than me. But I was the third chief editor in a row who had been appointed at roughly that sort of age, so people had got used to the idea of working for a younger boss. In a society like Japan where age counts for so much, such an idea is much more unusual. It is perhaps hard to say which it is that makes for more difficulty, being younger than your subordinates or being a woman. In Kono-san's case, she is both. But it seems to make very little difference.

Not that it has always been easy. 'When I started [as an executive officer], I had a lot of jealousy from men,' Kono-san told me. 'Now this is changing.' She is perfectly conscious of the fact that her success is unusual: 'When I got promotion, the men in my team said "congratulations". The women said "thank you",' she said, acknowledging her role as a pioneer 'building a new future for us women', demonstrating that women can be managers too. Her view of the differences between men and women: 'I think females are realistic thinkers compared with men; good at process and at project management. Men are more dreamers. Women tend to focus more on the short term, such as the next five years, whereas men are thinking of their whole careers.'

As Kono-san said, this may be because women assume they may not stay in their job for the long term and so focus on figuring out how to enjoy their current life and how to get on well with co-workers. This may also make them less tolerant of being given dead-end, unsatisfying jobs: compared with men, they see much less reason to endure a lousy job because they have less reason to think that such endurance is a price worth paying for long-term career benefits. For them, the long-term benefits may never come.

Actually, I interviewed Kono-san twice,[2] once when she had the rank of 'executive officer', and was already notable for being the most senior female in the Rakuten Group among forty people at that level, and then a second time shortly after she had been promoted to the top executive rank of the firm. That promotion made her the only woman at that level, as president of Rakuten Ichiba. Rakuten is a young company founded and managed by a very

---

[2] The second interview was also at Rakuten Crimson House, 2 March 2017.

strong-minded entrepreneur, Mikitani Hiroshi. In my first interview, Kono-san recognized that she (like other managers in the company) had to spend a lot of time receiving and responding to instructions from Mikitani-san. In fact, she said she would receive text messages from him at any hour of day or night. Unlike in a traditional company, she did not spend long hours working in the office. But she did work remotely from home, when necessary, which certainly included receiving Mikitani-san's directives.

In that first interview, Kono-san was quite down to earth and realistic about her role, relative to the big boss. 'I see myself as a kind of interpreter of his ideas,' she said. Her key skill, she thought, was communication, often taking Mikitani-san's orders and turning them into actions for her team to carry out. But by the time of our second interview several months later, when Kono-san had been promoted to an even higher responsibility, this habit of getting text messages late at night had stopped. He says 'we are synchronized,' so 'I no longer am an interpreter . . . . I have changed my mind about leadership since my promotion. Before, I was always waiting for my boss's direction. Now I have changed. I have to be a leader.'

Indeed she does: with those 3,500 people working for her, she has to be. With those larger responsibilities, she has had to learn different ways of managing. 'I used to use a micro-management style, paying attention to every detail. Now I have changed to the bigger picture, showing the team the basic directions.' As she says, Mikitani-san has delegated authority to her, so she must also delegate authority to others. They must be her interpreters.

I asked for examples. She gave one big example that she was clearly excited and pleased about. It concerned Rakuten's system of dealing with requests from customers for refunds for products they had bought but did not want, or wanted to change. The system had been slow and rather conservative: Rakuten was accepting only 20 per cent of the requests for refunds being passed on to them by merchants. Kono-san's biggest 'big picture' idea at Rakuten Ichiba is that she wants to make the service much more user-centred, giving such good experiences to customers that they come back to buy more. So she says she ordered Rakuten's teams of operators to increase the proportion of refund requests accepted from 20 per cent to 80 per cent, in the space of just one month, which sounds pretty ambitious. 'I didn't tell them how they should do this. I just told them to find the way themselves.' And they did: after just one month, the refund acceptance ratio had risen not just to 80 per cent but to 90 per cent.

How? The answer is simple. Before her change, operators received applications for refunds and then considered them carefully before giving the customer an answer, generally waiting for approval from senior staff. 'In Japan's complicated culture, people are always asking, asking, asking,' she said. Following Kono-san's new order, the operators altered the system radically. Now, they can accept the application immediately, in all but the most exceptional or unusual of cases and need only investigate later if something seems wrong. The operator themselves can make the decision, rather than needing to ask seniors, so they feel much more empowered. Instead of presuming customers asking for refunds are guilty in some way and need to be assessed, under the new system they are presumed to be innocent.

Sometimes, the image of a top manager is someone who is very driven, ambitious, tough and maybe even ruthless. That is far from the image that Kono-san conveys. She admits that subordinates often 'think that as I am the boss I must be very strict. But that means they don't know my personality.' Instead, the impression she says she wants to give is that she has a very open personality, and that she always wants information from the bottom up. She wants to come across as a good listener, in other words. But also, as Kono-san went on to say, 'quick decision-making is important from a leader.' The leader is the person responsible for making decisions, for making choices, but largely on the basis of information obtained from below.

Discipline matters too, for in a busy company there are a lot of people to meet and to listen to, and a lot of decisions to make. Kono-san declared to me, forcefully, that she has several rules of her own. One is that she has dinner with Rakuten people only a maximum of three times per month. Not for her the routine of evening dinner and drinking sessions. She says they 'can do communication in working hours. After working hours, I want to spend my time with external people.'

Another of her rules is that she says she wants to make sure she shares her thoughts and plans with two new people every day, whether in the company or external. Clearly, in her new job she travels a lot, both to represent the company and to meet sales teams; when we met in March 2017 she had just been sent a congratulation present of eighty roses by some of her team for her promotion but was worrying about how to keep them fresh given that she was due to go to Shizuoka the next day, and then on to Osaka.

Such discipline is clearly going to be necessary given the development that Kono-san told me about the third time[3] we met, on this occasion not for an interview but for a dinner hosted by the British Ambassador in Tokyo. Her first revelation was that she had added the role of Chief Marketing Officer to her duties. But then her second revelation was that she had just had a baby. She took two months' maternity leave, she said, and then returned to work. Asked about roles in the family, she simply answered by saying 'my husband is a good guy.'

Kono-san is an exceptional person, but then people who rise to top managerial jobs usually are. Her aptitude for business may well have derived from her family, for both of her parents ran businesses when she was young, her father as a consultant, her mother as a jewellery wholesaler. Perhaps not surprisingly, she even started her own small e-commerce business while she was studying at Aoyama Gakuin University, a business importing and selling Italian cosmetic products, a business she ran for five years, making a profit. She had her professor check the contracts her firm signed with overseas suppliers. Yet when she graduated she didn't carry on with that company, preferring instead to get some experience in marketing working for SBI Securities, a financial firm, joining Rakuten only when she was in her early 30s. But it is not surprising that Mikitani-san and his colleagues spotted her potential.

*   *   *

Higuchi Hiroe is also a manager of men, for whom communication skills are vital. In fact, she told[4] me that communication is the most

[3] 4 December 2019.
[4] Interview with Higuchi Hiroe, Shima Kanko Hotel, Kashikojima, Ise, 28 November 2017.

difficult aspect of her job. 'It is best not to be too casual' when talking with colleagues: 'You need a certain tension in the staff.' This is a person who speaks very softly and quietly, so softly that I find myself wondering whether her staff can always hear her. Why is tension needed, I asked? Her answer was that in her profession what is needed is strict concentration when working, to avoid minor injuries and minor failures. She has eighty people in all working for her, of which ten are in her own close team.

For Higuchi-san is an executive chef, running all the restaurant kitchens of the Shima Kanko hotel group at Kashikojima in Shima-City on the Ise Peninsula. She had her small moment of public attention in 2016 when Japan hosted the G7 summit of world leaders at her hotel, and she found herself cooking such local delicacies as abalone and *Ise-ebi* (Japanese spiny lobster) for Abe Shinzo, Barack Obama, Angela Merkel, and the other then leaders of the seven most advanced countries in the world.

To be a top chef is of course, first and foremost, about having great professional skills as a cook. But it is also a task of management, for every kitchen has to work like a well-drilled group of soldiers, working together to produce great cuisine under great pressure for a large number of people. The soft-spoken Higuchi-san says she 'understands that people think our kitchen is quieter than other kitchens. But when we have a lot of guests, it becomes like a battlefield.' To succeed on such a battlefield, it must be vital to be calm, but also to be a strong and clear communicator. In addition to running her own restaurant, as the hotel group's Executive Chef she has to give overall direction and management to all the other restaurants in the Shima Kanko group, each of which has a team of cooks led by one top chef. All of those other top chefs are men. Apart from Higuchi-san herself, there are just two other female chefs in the group, though there are a number of female patissiers.

On that cooking battlefield, Higuchi-san told me, what is needed most is physical strength and toughness, which is one reason why relatively few women stay on as chefs in the long term. Out of ten female colleagues with her at cooking school, she said that only two are still working as cooks. As well as her good health and toughness, she said she also needed the understanding of the people around her while she was raising her two children. By this she meant first of all her family members, but also her colleagues at work. If her child got ill making her have to pick them up from school, for example, other members of staff would fill in for her. Higuchi-san said she thought that even the male chefs did this because as they also had children they could understand the pressures. I imagine also they knew that Higuchi-san was a hard worker, who would make up for any lost time and return the favour if they needed it. She is nothing if not a team-player.

The most important part of her story is perhaps Higuchi-san's relationship with her husband. Originally, he also worked at the Shima-Kanko hotel as a chef, but he gave up that work and left it to her, as, she says, 'he knew how much I loved cooking.' He is now working as a driver of delivery trucks for goods. I asked whether he cooks for the family at home: 'sometimes', she said with a smile. They have two sons, who at the time of our interview in 2017 were aged 16 and 13. Higuchi-san says that when they were smaller she always returned home to cook their dinner, but now she often doesn't see them at all in the evening as she likes to work at the hotel every dinner-time. In principle she has eight days holiday each month but she says she often takes fewer as she loves working.

Clearly, Higuchi-san is someone who enjoys being an executive chef. But she says that what is now enabling more female chefs to work and to succeed is an improvement in their working environment. Today, she says, chefs have more control over their working hours, can have a secure number of holidays, and no longer need to work from early morning until late at night. Higuchi-san says that she hopes to stay working as a chef for the rest of her life but is still conscious of the need to create a work environment in which it is easy for others to work, whether they are men or women.

When she was promoted to become executive chef, some of the experienced male chefs must have felt a bit jealous. 'When I changed from being a junior to become the boss, I realized this was difficult for men [in my staff] who had more experience than me, who had maybe even been already here when I joined,' she said. I asked Higuchi-san how she overcame this. She said it was 'difficult'. But she says she realized that if she was too reserved vis-à-vis her male colleagues then that would not be good either, as it would hinder communication. She says she tried to use polite, careful words with the men when giving them instructions. How about when things go wrong, I asked? She said she tries to hold a real and open discussion in front of the whole group on why failures have happened. In all cases, she said, both creativity and clear management of staff are important for an executive chef.

*   *   *

Walking into[5] Art Corporation's very smart new headquarters in Osaka, with rooms and corridors lined with congratulatory displays of flowers, I was reminded of how different the company's offices had been when I first met Terada Chiyono, the president of the firm. Back then, they were quite small and humble, if I remember correctly—which I may not do, since that first meeting took place more than thirty years earlier, in 1986 when I was based in Tokyo as a foreign correspondent for *The Economist*.

I wrote an article at that time that was headlined 'Three to watch of the new generation', was published on 1 February 1986, and which reported on three small, entrepreneurial businesses that had caught my eye which I thought might interest our foreign readers. Western readers in those days tended to associate Japan just with famous firms like Panasonic, Toyota, and Sony, so I wanted to let them know that this wasn't the whole story. I visited a fast-growing restaurant chain, MOS Burger, and talked to its founder Sakurada Satoshi about his ambitions. I visited a computer software company called Ascii Corporation, whose founder Nishi Kazuhiko had struck up a friendship with Microsoft's Bill Gates and had big plans in the computer business. And I visited *Art Hikkoshi Center* (Art Removals Centre), my ears full of the firm's catchy advertising tunes, my eyes drawn by the extremely unusual fact that their president was a then 39-year-old woman, Terada Chiyono.

The Terada family had had a small goods-haulage company when, in 1976, Terada-san suggested to her husband, who was the boss, that they should shift into the home removals business in

[5] Interview with Terada Chiyono, Art Corporation Head Office, Osaka, 6 July 2017.

order to make a bigger, more profitable venture. He was apparently sceptical but agreed to the proposal on condition that she should run the new firm. A decade later, in 1986 when I visited, the removals firm had become a lot larger than the haulage business and the husband was working for his wife. At that time, the Teradas' business held 3 per cent of the home removals market in Japan. When I visited the company for the second time, in 2017, the firm by then enjoyed 25 per cent of the removals market. And Terada-san, by then 70 years old, was still running the business and has become one of the Kansai[6] region's most well-known managers.

As she told me, she had by then been working for fifty years in the transport business and forty-one since the foundation of *Art Hikkoshi Center*. She sounded joyful about having done the same work for half a century. 'I don't feel the length of years, so far,' she said. 'Will you still be working at 80?', I asked. 'No, of course not!' she replied, 'I want to have time to kill.' At that time, I felt sure she would not retire any time soon. But her two sons were working in Art Corporation in senior positions, learning all about it. She expressed the hope that 'at least to their generation, Art will be a Terada company.' And sure enough, on 20 December 2019 Terada-san formally retired from her role as president of Art Corporation, becoming honorary chair as well as president of Art Group Holdings. Her eldest son, Terada Masato, succeeded her as president of Art Corporation.

Asked about how it was to have her husband working for her, Terada-san is clear-minded and realistic: 'My husband and I were different in what we were good at in work, but we had a common dream to make the company bigger. That's how it worked.' It is certainly not conventional for a husband to concede corporate leadership—and a far bigger public profile—to his wife, but that is what has happened during the more than fifty years that this couple have worked together in this family business. 'I have never felt that being a woman is an issue. And when one is working, I haven't really felt that there is any difference between men and women.'

---

[6] Kansai is the region around Osaka in western Japan.

Nevertheless, in 2010, personal and family issues did come to the fore, in ways that Terada-san acknowledges did damage to the business: this was when her husband's personal behaviour led to a sexual scandal and court case. Had this happened in 2018, the media would surely have compared it to the disgrace of Harvey Weinstein in the United States, for like the US Hollywood mogul, Mr Terada was shown to have used the incentive of a career in films and advertising as a means to induce teenage girls to have sex with him, for which he paid them.

The question that this sordid and disgraceful story raises is not, at least not directly, the behaviour of Mr Terada himself. The real issue is a familiar one for women in politics, though perhaps less so for women in business: should a wife be held responsible, in any way, for the sins of her husband? For that question, Harvey Weinstein is not the relevant foreign comparison but rather Bill Clinton, for his wife Hilary Rodham Clinton has had to face questions and reputational damage for years now over her attitude to the sexual sins of her husband, most notably his affair with a White House intern, Monica Lewinsky, when he was president.

The simple answer ought to be: No, the wife should not be held responsible for, or really even tainted, by the sins of the husband, any more than a male chief executive or political leader should be held responsible if his wife were to have a sexual affair. The problem for Terada-san and for Art Corporation has, however, been that the solution to a family problem becomes a lot less simple when we are talking about a family owned or controlled business. That is why, when I asked her about how her husband's sexual scandal had affected the firm, she replied 'For a company facing consumers, although it was nothing to do with the services we provide, we cannot deny that our reputation was diminished and our business was affected because such a case happened.'

Once such an event has happened, the key question becomes how the company and its chief executive responds. She said:

We made it clear where responsibility lies by the fact that the person responsible [that is, Mr Terada] resigned from his post [as chairman]. In addition, I submitted my resignation from my position as an independent director at other organizations such as other companies or economic associations. However, I was persuaded to stay, as those organizations concluded that the problem was not one of Terada Chiyono herself.

All that sounds reasonable and appropriate. More controversial was the fact that having resigned as chairman, the husband later returned. Terada-san justifies this by pointing out his status and importance as one of the founders of the company. In the end, this is a family question in a family business—had the couple divorced as a result of the scandal, perhaps he would not have returned to the company, but as they decided to remain married, the idea of him still having an influential role in the family company is not surprising.

Family issues are never easy for a female corporate leader. As well as a wayward husband, there is the issue of bringing up children. Terada-san waves this to one side, however, in typically forthright fashion: she told me that she never felt that having children affected the speed with which she and her husband were able to develop the business. She admits (as many working mothers do) that it is possible that her running and expanding the business could have had negative effects on her children, but I suspect she does not believe it was so. In fact, she added that she believes her sons learned a lot by watching what their parents were doing. One quite common theme among the women I talked to who are now in management positions is that their parents have often been in business themselves. Thinking about management and business may come more naturally to them than to others.

Terada-san has become such an iconic figure, over a very long period, that she is often asked for advice by younger women about starting or running their own businesses. She is strikingly critical of the young women she talks to, but in a constructive way. She told me that 'while there are now many women who have started their own businesses or would like to, they often do so really as a kind of hobby turned into a small company.' Rather than there being any particular obstacles standing in the way of these female entrepreneurs, Terada-san thinks 'the issue lies in women's minds, in their lack of ambition and real targets.' She says that the women she meets 'often praise me for my success, but they don't talk much about what they really want their companies to become. They don't draw a future plan or picture for their company.'

This recalls something the great Austrian-American management writer Peter Drucker used to say: that every corporate leader needs to have 'a theory of their business', a conception of why it can work, of what its purpose is, and where they wish to take it. Terada-san is right that every business leader, whether male or female, needs to have such a theory in their minds, with an ambitious plan based on realistic research.

Certainly, during the more than thirty years between our two meetings, Terada-san's plans have changed many times, but her basic ambition and theory of the business has not. One ambition that she told me about during our 1986 meeting soon had to be scrapped: this was an expansion of the business into the United States. This idea was no doubt a product of the bubble era and of the widespread belief that with valuable yen in their hands, Japanese companies could enter and conquer foreign markets. The American business turned out, in fact, to really just consist of removals between Japan and the United States, and efforts to build a domestic US business did not work well.

Other plans led the firm to make a public flotation of its shares on the stockmarket in 2004 to raise capital and, as she describes it, to provide rewards for employees after a long period of good growth. But after four years as a public company, Terada-san changed her mind and borrowed enough money to take the firm private again the following year. She explains this decision by saying that as a public company Art Corporation found itself spending all its time on short-term targets rather than on pursuing dreams: they were focusing too much on the trees and not enough on the forest. As she put it, they realized that they did not in fact need new capital from the market, as they were profitable enough to finance expansion from their retained earnings. It cost a lot to buy the shareholders out, but the firm paid back all the loans in 2016 and so now has zero debt.

All firms have to try things, but then abandon them if they don't work. In the case of Art Corporation, this did not damage or badly affect the long-term plan of expanding the removals business as a premium service, as a proposition to support households in every aspect of moving house. Now, that business faces some fundamental demographic challenges: the slow decline in Japan's population could mean a slow decline in the household removals business too.

I asked Terada-san about this challenge. She pointed out that when Art was a small firm, the typical Japanese household contained four people, but now it had fallen to three or less. The number of households has not yet declined, although she expects that this will happen quite soon. The size of the market will be shrinking, but so will be the manpower available to work in the removals business. In response to changing demography, but also to the changing needs and expectations of mothers, Terada-san has made a big new investment in recent years: starting in 2005, Art Corporation has established, partly through organic growth and partly through acquisition, a subsidiary company running 180 nursery schools.

This is a theme which will return in Chapter 5. Nursery schools, or daycare centres as some call them, are a big growth business—or at least, there is growing demand for them, as more mothers work and as there has also been an increase in the number of single mothers. Terada-san said that Art's is the country's fourth-largest nursery school business, with 123 of its schools taking children privately and 57 doing so via approval by local authorities who in return provide public subsidies to parents and regulate pricing. That regulated pricing, along with a shortage of qualified teachers, forms the biggest problem for this business. But Art's nursery school company nevertheless has annual sales of Y7 billion and Terada-san said the aim is to reach Y10 billion.

This still makes the business very much a junior partner to removals, which accounted in the 2017 fiscal year for 64.1 per cent of group sales that totalled Y100 billion. The rest comes from commercial goods distribution, from commodity sales, from real estate, and from the nursery school business. Their hope is to expand those other businesses sufficiently to make the split 50-50 between removals and the rest. That is very much the watchword of Terada Chiyono as a company president: always to have a plan, an ambition, a dream. That is what makes the difference, as she says, between a successful entrepreneur and a hobbyist.

5

Starting Something New

Fish Toko Atsuko, Hayashi Chiaki, Mitarai Tamako,
and Nakamura Noriko

Leadership is a difficult skill to learn. It comes naturally to only a few people, but otherwise has to be learned by experience, generally by having the chance to lead small groups of people at lower levels in a company and then rising to more senior positions that carry broader responsibilities. One of the difficulties for women in the past has been that as outsiders in mainly male-run organizations they have found it difficult to build up that sort of experience. Traditional schools and families have also provided boys with more chances to learn how to lead than girls. Given all those disadvantages, often the best option for women who do want to exercise leadership is to start their own new businesses, either as non-profits or for-profits. Having your own enterprise is certainly a way to create your own reality, rather than needing to fit in to somebody else's. But doing so is hardly easy, either, and is quite rare in Japan, both for men and for women: Goldman Sachs reports,[1] citing the Global Entrepreneurship Monitor of 2018–19, that only 4 per cent of Japanese women and 6.7 per cent of men take part in entrepreneurial activity.

That is why programmes such as the Japanese Women's Leadership Initiative[2] that was started in 2006 by Fish Toko Atsuko are so important and welcome. Fish-san lives in Boston, Massachusetts, with her American banker husband, and began the programme using funds from their Fish Family Foundation. They bring a group

---

[1] Goldman Sachs, 16 April 2019, p. 23.   [2] https://jwli.org.

of young women to Boston every year from Japan on fellowships to help them to learn about leadership and how to start and develop an enterprise. Initially, Fish-san told[3] me, the programme did not get a good response: corporate Japan did not want to see or support any change; the Japanese government 'saw us as a foreign activist' attuned chiefly to humanitarian issues such as refugees and women's rights; and applicants in the early years did not have a very clear idea about what they wanted to do or could do.

She thinks things really began to change after the 3/11 earthquake and tsunami, because social enterprises and civil society groups became more widely accepted, reported upon in the media, and admired. Now, Fish-san says that applicants come with clearer ideas and are more confident about what they can do. Successful fellows—generally four to six people each year—are brought to Boston for a four-week stay, where they are helped to develop an action plan and receive mentoring about their project and their personal style, and then over the next two years their progress is tracked, and reports are submitted for scrutiny and advice every six months.

Clearly, the women who go to Boston have to be those who can already speak English, for much of the mentoring and guidance is done by English-speakers. It is therefore a selection from a particular group of wannabe leaders. But that group is not as untypical as it may sound: the number of young Japanese women who can speak English is higher than the number of men in the same age-group as more female students go abroad for study or work experience than males.

Nowadays, the main focus of the Japanese Women's Leadership Initiative is social change, so most of the fellows have plans for non-profit organizations rather than business start-ups. Such social enterprises are not so different from for-profit start-ups, especially in the need for leadership, for a clear sense of purpose, and for highly disciplined management, even though they don't make their founders wealthy. They can however enter for a new award that

---

[3] Interview with Fish Toko Atsuko, JWLI offices, Boston, Massachusetts, 18 October 2017.

Fish-san has launched, as can other Japanese social and private entrepreneurs: it is called the Champions of Change award and carries with it prize money donated by the Fish Foundation of $10,000. As Baba-san said in Chapter 3, prize money can be helpful during a business's launch phase, as can be the publicity that comes with an award.

One person who has often given talks to the JWLI fellows and has acted as a mentor, however, is a young woman whose career path looks very much like that of a typical American entrepreneur. She is Hayashi Chiaki, co-founder of a consultancy firm called Loftwork, and Fish-san introduced me to her.

*   *   *

Hayashi-san and I met[4] in one of her company's ventures, the FabCafe in Shibuya, in Tokyo. The café is full of quite large and impressive machines that can be used for 3-D printing: hence the name 'fab', being short for fabrication. Customers can pay to use the machines to build products, generally design-prototypes and models, which accounts for about one-third of FabCafe's income. Another third comes from food and beverages, while the remainder comes from leasing the space to companies who want to connect with (and promote their products or services to) the community of designers and developers who use FabCafe. The essential point of the business is to develop that community.

Her company now has three FabCafes in Japan and eight overseas, in cities such as Singapore, Bangkok, Barcelona, and even Monterey. Why so many overseas, I asked? To build collaborative networks of people and ideas, Hayashi-san said, all around the world, so that the Japanese designer community in their network is also well-connected to world-class thinking. FabCafes are typically set up with local partners, so clearly the determinant of each next opening is whether a local partner emerges. The furthest away is in Monterey in Mexico where a family owns and runs the café. The mother there is a well-known professor of innovation, and she sent

---

[4] Interview with Hayashi Chiaki, FabCafe Shibuya, Tokyo, 1 December 2017.

her son and daughter to Tokyo for two months to get to know FabCafe and its parent firm, Loftwork,[5] a creative agency.

What felt especially notable about Hayashi-san was the sense she gave of having taken personal control of her career and life, ultimately by co-founding her Loftwork business but even before then too. A graduate of Waseda University, her first job was marketing cosmetics for Kao Corporation in 1994–7. She had to do research on women and their feelings about life and work, and says she found that many were under high levels of stress, especially about their difficulties in finding a fulfilling job. Clearly, selling cosmetics to use on your skin was dealing with the symptoms rather than any underlying issues. For her own development, Hayashi-san decided to quit and become a business journalist instead.

To do that, despite not speaking much English at that time, she chose to apply to American journalism schools because she felt that 'in Japan, almost all "future stories" come from the US,' so she wanted to go and see part of that future. She was particularly interested in the changes coming to work and life from technology. Only able to finance a one-year masters programme from her savings, she chose to apply for such programmes at Boston University, at Columbia in New York, and at Wisconsin-Madison, ending up in Boston.

When she graduated from there she applied only for jobs in New York, feeling that that city was a centre of change, and joined the Kyodo News Agency as an assistant. At that time, the agency's business journalists were busy following the 1990s dotcom boom of internet-related start-ups on the NASDAQ technology stock exchange, so she too spent her time chasing around start-ups, press conferences, and the like. After a year doing that, she decided to apply for a job at AERA, the Asahi newspaper's weekly magazine. She believed, she said, that the daily Asahi was read only by old people and followers of the baseball results, while AERA was being read by younger people. But disappointment followed, which led to inspiration. As she said to me: 'I didn't get the job I wanted. So I did

---

[5] https://loftwork.com/en/people/?whr=tokyo.

what a lot of people around me said I should do: start a business, with a group of friends.'

The business, launched in 2000, was (and is) Loftwork. It is a design consultancy which has established a large network of creators and designers who form teams for particular projects, which earn a commission for the company. Now, Loftwork has more than 150 of its own employees in ten locations around the world, says its associates have worked on more than 55,000 projects and boasts of a network of more than 30,000 creators and designers. Initially, like some American start-ups at the time, Loftwork hosted a website on which creators could post their portfolios and pitch for work. Now, it is involved more in project management, organizing teams, brainstorming among the network, and acting as a kind of infrastructure for creativity.

Meeting someone like Hayashi-san in New York or London would seem fairly commonplace. Today's digital, networked economy has spawned a lot of companies like Loftwork in Europe and America, ones which work with a wide group of self-employed individuals and small firms. But this sort of company, and this sort of entrepreneurial leader, feels rarer in a country like Japan where the notion of 'disruption' by technological change and new business models has been resisted more successfully by old established companies. In Hayashi-san's story, however, one thing that is clear is the sense of autonomy, flexibility, and connectedness that she gains from this sort of firm and this sort of life.

Connected is an important watchword: Hayashi-san is also the Japan Liaison for the famous Media Lab at Massachusetts Institute of Technology, the world's best academic centre on these issues. The Media Lab was directed from 2011–19[6] by a Japanese innovator, Ito Joichi ('Joi'), who has had his own very varied career in technology, entrepreneurship, and academia, partly in America and partly in Japan and is also a shareholder in Loftwork. About twenty of the eighty corporate sponsors of the MIT Media Lab are Japanese firms,

---

[6] Ito Joichi resigned as director on 7 September 2019 after it emerged that the sexual offender Jeffrey Epstein had made large donations to the Media Lab as well as investing in Ito's own venture funds.

so Hayashi-san organizes events and other community-building activities for them in Tokyo and other Japanese cities.

She told me of another interesting idea about connectedness, one which concerns not tech firms but older people. It is that, based on research she and a team have been doing over the past two years, financed by the Japanese government and a consortium of private companies, she thinks that women over the age of 65 tend to be better connected with other people (especially other women) than are elderly men. This makes older women more able and willing to engage in projects and to form social enterprises than men are, she finds. Men, by contrast, had their all their connections inside the companies by which they were employed until retirement, and so have weaker connections in the wider world once they have retired.

* * *

In Kesennuma in Miyagi prefecture in Tohoku during a visit[7] in November 2016 I saw just that sort of connectedness among older women on display. Seated around a large table were about twenty women actually of all ages, but with a number who seemed to be at around or after what in the formal economy is known as 'retirement age'. It is doubtful however that many of these women or their menfolk had worked in the sort of companies which have retirement ages and pension schemes. For this is a fishing community, sadly well known both in Japan and internationally thanks to the devastation caused by the 3/11 earthquake and tsunami, and many of these women are married to fishermen. They come together in this studio for work, which they are doing on a self-employed basis but on contract to a company whose female chief executive or president is there, in the studio, giving out instructions and guidance. She was just 31 years old when I visited. Looking at the group of workers, it was impossible to avoid thinking that many of the group would be old enough to be that chief executive's mother or even grandmother.

Nevertheless, undaunted by the difference in ages, that young company president spoke to the group in a strict but friendly way.

[7] Interviews with Mitarai Tamako, Kesennuma, Miyagi Prefecture, 30 November and 1 December 2016.

She spoke about a recent promotional event in Kyoto which had led to strong sales, a message which drew applause from the assembled team. She told a story of one customer's admiration for the way in which the product she had bought from the firm had got better and fitted better over the three years during which she had owned it. Enduring quality, the chief executive emphasized, is essential to what they are offering, a type of quality which means that their products must have a long life-cycle, maturing over time in such a way that unlike with other goods it is not a question simply of the product having been in its peak condition when it was in the shop and deteriorating thereafter. The young president finished by introducing to her team the book she is reading, which is about a master craftsman and his thinking. That, this exercise in leadership was intended to convey, is the way we should think too.

As I later told Mitarai Tamako, the young president to whom I was listening, the more I learned about her company, Kesennuma Knitting, the more I thought about an Italian entrepreneur whom I had visited[8] in his beautiful small town in Umbria, in central Italy, a few years earlier. He is Brunello Cuccinelli, and I thought of him because what Kesennuma Knitting has achieved is quite similar to what he has done, although on a smaller scale. This is that by emphasizing the very high quality of her firm's handmade sweaters and cardigans Mitarai-san has managed to achieve what by any standards are extraordinarily high prices.

Anyone who has stepped through the door of one of Mr Cuccinelli's stores in Milan, London, New York, or Tokyo will know that while his mainly cashmere garments are exquisite and are handmade by his group of seamstresses in Italy, the prices are so high as to make your eyes water. To me, to pay Y150,000 (a little over £1,100 or $1,400) for a made-to-order cardigan from Kesennuma called MM01 would be equally eye-watering. But at the time I visited, the firm had a waiting list of two hundred customers and each cardigan was taking two years to make and deliver. Those who want something even more exclusive can pay Y190,000 for a special limited edition, a colourful patterned sweater called Rhythm-A.

---

[8] For my book *Good Italy, Bad Italy* (Yale University Press, 2012).

But, as Mitarai-san was saying to her team, what Kesennuma Knitting is offering is not just a simple garment: it is a whole experience of having the garment made to measure and to order for each customer, and then the experience of using this garment over its whole lifetime.

In the years immediately after the disaster, people's willingness to pay such high prices could sometimes be explained by their sense of charity and desire to show solidarity with a devastated community. But welcome as it is, such willingness does not typically last long enough to make a business sustainable. Many social enterprises that were set up in Tohoku after the disaster have long since closed. The fact that now, nine years after the tragedy, Kesennuma Knitting is a thriving, profitable business that is taking in lots of orders for its high-quality, high-priced sweaters and cardigans shows that charity and solidarity are not the explanation. Smart marketing has to be part of the answer, just as it is with Brunello Cuccinelli. So must be the quality of the product and the experience of buying it.

Certainly, if Terada Chiyono of Art Corporation were to meet Tamako Mitarai she would be impressed by this young female entrepreneur's vision for her company and by her ambition. I asked Mitarai-san what future she saw for Kesennuma Knitting and her answer was that she wants to establish a company that can last one hundred or two hundred years, just like the best craftsmanship-based companies in the past.

Young though she is, she obviously doesn't expect to remain in charge all that time (and being single at present, she has no children able in principle to turn this into a family business). She says she feels the need to build the company to the sort of level from which it will be possible to hand it over to a second president, who would be likely to be someone from outside, she says. Asked how big the company could grow, she said it could grow to double or treble its current output, but not ten times as large. Personally, I think the precedent of Brunello Cuccinelli's success in building a larger company that is still based on hand-made products by his team of seamstresses suggests that Kesennuma Knitting could potentially expand by more than she was saying. But to treble output would still be a major expansion.

One remarkable feature of Kesennuma Knitting is that until Mitarai-san came to Tohoku and started the company, she knew little about knitting or about the clothing business. She came because she was recruited by a well-known advertising copywriter, game designer, and writer, Itoi Shigesato,[9] who had the idea to try to start some local enterprises to help heal and revive damaged communities after the tsunami. Itoi-san had apparently been reading a blog Mitarai-san had been writing about Bhutan, high in the Himalayas, and was impressed by the way she observed and connected both with the people there and with her readers. So he picked her for Kesennuma Knitting as a good communicator but also as someone who, intriguingly perhaps, had learned about business while working for the McKinsey management consultancy in Tokyo.

That is the unusual path that led her to Kesennuma: from a famous global consulting firm to Miyagi Prefecture, via Bhutan. She must have seemed quite a strange creature to the community in Kesennuma in 2011–12, but it was a time when a lot of outsiders arrived, offering their help. Mitarai-san took a home-stay with a local family rather than taking over a house or apartment given that housing was scarce thanks to the tsunami. In fact, when I visited in late 2016 she was still living with that same family and the showroom Kesennuma Knitting opened in the town to be able to show its products to visiting customers is in a property owned by the family. She speaks with pleasure about feeling that she had become part of the community when she was invited to take part in a local festival, playing taiko drums which she had been practising for several months. They thought of her, she says, as just 'a young girl who had come to live in Kesennuma'.

My impression of Mitarai-san is that she is certainly talented, especially at leadership, but is also level-headed. Her background is that she went to a girls-only private school and came from a family in which both of her parents worked in business. Her father ran his own metal-processing company in which he had succeeded another family owner, and her mother worked at a Seibu Department store as a merchandiser. Her mother later started her own company

[9] https://en.wikipedia.org/wiki/Shigesato_Itoi.

doing consultancy for department stores and other retailers about merchandising. The family environment was therefore unusually busy, as well as business-oriented, which meant that her mother liked to send young Tamako and her other two children away to camps in the summer. Those summer camps, which were often abroad, play an important part in the way Mitarai-san talks about herself, her international awareness and the development of her leadership skills.

Her first international summer camp took place in Portugal. She was 11 years old, and went as a member of a Japanese delegation (one of twelve countries). The camp was organized by an American non-profit, CISV[10] (which stands for Children's International Summer Villages). Before attending she says she spoke no English and so found it hard to make friends, but by the end of the month-long camp she clearly had broken through that barrier and had had what she describes as a formative and strong experience. Four years later she asked her mother to send her to another CISV camp, this time in Germany. As this was for 15-year-olds it was a somewhat more adult experience, which meant that the teenage attendees were given more responsibility for managing their own schedules and the camp itself. Mitarai-san says she found it very different from the one in Portugal four years earlier, with many of the campers a lot less motivated. No doubt there were a fair number of grumpy and moody teenagers, along with some who were unruly, drank alcohol, and even went outside the camp and got arrested.

They had a camp meeting every day to discuss rules and plans, and halfway through her time there Mitarai-san was elected by the other attendees as chairman of the whole camp. It was a difficult task, she says, but she learned a lot from it, especially about the need to recognize a diversity of values and approaches in different cultures and even just differences between people. Her subsequent career, and what was evident in the Kesennuma Knitting studio, show that she had the instincts and qualities of leadership at an early age, as well as a mind that is quite organized and disciplined.

---

[10] https://cisv.org.

While Mitarai-san says she had something of a philanthropic cast of mind in her late teens, she decided to try to gear herself up for an economic or business-like approach to such social objectives by applying to the University of Tokyo and studying economics there. As one of the fairly small number of female students there she says she felt 'the power of being a minority' as she could get others to look after her.

Life was different when she graduated and got a job with McKinsey in Tokyo where gender equality was taken more seriously. Mitarai-san says she felt equal to the men there, but it was nevertheless a very masculine environment in which she felt she 'needed to behave like a man'. Her friends told her she had 'sold out' by joining a firm like McKinsey. But she felt, as many others before her have done both in Japan and in other countries, that joining the firm offered a fast way to learn about business decision-making, giving even a junior staffer quick connections to executives.

She worked there for just two years and three months before an opportunity came up in Bhutan which she decided to grab. It arose thanks to McKinsey's Delhi office, as the government of Bhutan approached them looking for a consultant willing to work in Bhutan for a year helping them work out how to develop their tourism industry. This was offered to Mitarai-san, she says, because she was known to be interested in social fields but also because her boss in Tokyo thought that if she were to go off and spend that year in Bhutan satisfying her social instincts she might afterwards return to the firm and stay for longer.

That was indeed her plan, after what she describes as 'a life-changing experience' in Bhutan—a place where women were more common in professional jobs than was the case in Tokyo. In Japan and at McKinsey, she says, she felt work was quite separated from people's daily lives whereas in Bhutan the two felt more symbiotic: work was just part of life. I suspect this is what she has now managed to create for herself in Kesennuma Knitting, a life where the line between work and other daily issues doesn't really exist. She expected to go back to McKinsey for a lot more years, but then 3/11 occurred, changing her frame of mind and leading also to the offer by Itoi-san of setting up a knitting firm, using traditional skills of women there.

As is shown by the high prices for Kesennuma Knitting's sweaters, the firm has ended up doing a lot more than just using traditional skills. Women who come to work for the firm spend a long period training and practising so as to reach a professional quality—a quality of work that Mitarai-san's firm has successfully developed and enhanced. They use the finest wools: merino from Spain, the wool of the Blue-Faced Leicester and Cheviot sheep from England. A new knitter typically takes three to six months to complete their first sweater, and it is usually not saleable. If a knitter makes a mistake, they unravel the wool and reknit it, but they are allowed to do that only a maximum of three times as the wool has a different feel if it is reknit too many times.

In the studio, I watched as Mitarai-san made quality checks on the sweaters, in front of the class of knitters: she laid them out on the table, felt all over them with her hands, and studied them visually with her head right down at table level, so as to be able to see any flaws. As my visit was during the winter, I heard her explain to the group how important it is to keep the yarn away from heat sources such as the traditional *Kotatsu* under-table brazier, as the heat will affect the yarn by changing its water content.

It is demanding work, but also rewarding at many levels. I spoke to one of the instructors, Tamura-san. She had lost two family members during the tsunami and her house was destroyed. She said that after 3/11 she found it very difficult to spend time with other people who had not been affected in the same way, which is one reason why the knitting groups worked so well: they brought together people who had lived through the same disaster. She pointed out that Mitarai-san is the same age as her daughter and that at first she had thought she was very young. But then she saw that she had good international sense and experience.

One defining characteristic of the company is the way in which the knitters themselves are put in touch with the customers. Each garment carries a label with a small, rather sweet, cartoon-like drawing of the knitter who made it. During the preparation period, the knitter communicates with the customer who is placing the order so as to get the right measurements, and photos are sent showing each stage of the process. Some customers post those photos on social media, providing excellent free advertising for the company.

Mitarai-san is not just an employee of the company. She also owns 40 per cent of the shares. When Kesennuma Knitting was founded, it relied on support from Itoi-san's company, so his office owned 20 per cent of the equity, he owned 40 per cent personally, and Mitarai-san took 40 per cent. Now, because Itoi-san's company was floated on the stockmarket he decided that to have both a corporate shareholding and a personal one would be a conflict of interest, so he sold his 40 per cent share to the owner of a Hokkaido-based retailing and confectionary company, Rokka-tei.

I asked what advice Mitarai-san gives to younger people to whom she finds herself giving lectures at schools and universities. She said that her advice to kids is that what matters is 'not what you want to be, but how you want to be'. In other words, think about what your philosophy is, what kind of person you want to be, before you think about what skills to learn or jobs to seek.

Will the role of women increase in Japan in the future? This felt a natural question to ask of a young woman who has found and created her own path. Her answer was that the role of women will certainly increase, but not because of men deciding to empower them. It would increase because everyone in society will find that women are needed. As that develops, so women will emerge, thought Mitarai-san, into leadership positions, by a natural process.

*   *   *

One such woman emerged thirty years ago following a short career as an announcer at TV Asahi.[11] Nakamura Noriko had joined TV Asahi when she graduated but then after three years followed the then normal path of getting married, having a baby, and quitting her job. She says[12] that 'I stayed at home for three years after having my baby but I had so much energy that I couldn't stay as a housewife forever.' TV Asahi offered her the chance to come back on a

---

[11] A TV company affiliated with the Asahi Shimbun (daily newspaper) company.

[12] Interview with Nakamura Noriko and Todoroki Maiko, Poppins Head Office, Hiroo, Tokyo, 17 May 2018.

short-term contract but she felt the irregular hours were not going to work with a young child. Her own experience in trying to find babysitters to look after 3-year-old Maiko gave her a business idea, which in turn blended with an earlier idea she had had when she left TV Asahi.

The new idea was to start her own company to supply babysitters to hard-pressed parents, launching it in 1987 under the name Poppins. This name was of course taken from the famous children's book about a nanny, *Mary Poppins* by Pamela Travers, a British writer of the 1930s, which Disney had turned into a popular film in 1964. And the earlier idea that this became blended with was her decision in 1985 to set up a Japan Association for Female Executives,[13] to promote networking and provide support for female professionals of many kinds. Since there were then not very many female executives at all, this was quite a pioneering move. She thus became dedicated through both an association and a company to supporting working women.

Now, more than three decades later, that baby Maiko has become Todoroki Maiko (Todoroki is her married name) and is working as President and CEO of Poppins alongside her mother as founder and Chairperson. Their company is Japan's largest supplier of trained nannies, as well as being one of its top operators of nursery schools or daycare centres with more than 210 such facilities. The firm has also branched out into providing care services for elderly people. The company's headquarters in Hiroo in Tokyo is very smart, clean, and modern, and as far as I could tell is mainly staffed by women. It is a family business supplying services to families.

Well, actually, it is also increasingly supplying services to companies, who in turn provide them for the families of their staff. This is an important sign of accelerating change in corporate and institutional Japan. Looking at Poppins's openings of new nursery schools year by year over the past decade you can see both that the pace of growth has increased sharply—twelve new schools in each of 2009 and 2010, but then twenty-seven new schools in 2017 and twenty-three in 2018—and that more of them are being opened on behalf

[13] http://www.jafe.jp/en/.

of companies and universities. In 2018, seventeen of the twenty-three were opened for companies and one for the University of Tokyo; in 2017, thirteen of the twenty-seven were for companies.

A similar indication can be seen in Poppins's nanny business, which operates principally in Tokyo, Kyoto, and Osaka. This is a high-priced service which has always chiefly been of interest to, and affordable by, affluent families. Nakamura-san explained that they offer three kinds of nanny service: a premium contract, under which nannies are provided for Y2,800 per hour for a minimum of three hours; a standard contract at Y2,500 per hour; and a corporate contract which offers support to mothers that may be needed urgently, at short notice (for example because a child is ill). These corporate contracts, Nakamura-san and her daughter Todoroki-san told me, are surging in number: the firm had 380 such contracts in 2017 and by May 2018 had more than 500. These are not just for private firms: Poppins also has a contract with Tokyo Metropolitan Police, for among that agency's 43,500 police 4,100 are females, a proportion which the agency aims to increase. That contract Nakamura-san described to me as 'manna from heaven' as it led to about six other local police agencies taking out contracts. Through Japan Post, they are also building up contracts with some of the country's 24,000 local post offices.

This rise in the supply of childcare facilities is crucial if women are to be able to combine careers and motherhood. As was noted in Chapter 2, Prime Minister Abe promised a big expansion in childcare facilities including nursery schools; while that big expansion has duly occurred, there is still a gap between supply and demand. The chief obstacle, as both Nakamura-san and Terada-san of Art Corporation said, is a shortage of nursery-school teachers.

Nakamura-san says she has been fighting for all sorts of regulations to be relaxed throughout her thirty years in the business, and now one of her main complaints is over the very restrictive rules on how a nursery-school teacher must be qualified, generally either after two years at a specialized college or as postgraduates, largely from junior colleges, who can take a national test. Only 14 per cent of those pass the exam. There are 669 specialized colleges producing about 35,000 graduates each year, but less than half end up working as teachers in nursery schools. Competition from other, better paid jobs lures the others away. Nakamura-san says she is trying to get approval to bring in as teachers people who have related experience rather than the normal qualification. She is also trying to persuade the government to introduce a tax deduction for the use of baby-sitting services, which would make it more afford-able for working mothers as well as encouraging more mothers to stay in work rather than becoming full-time housewives.

Poppins takes as its model for its nanny service a long-established and highly respected British school, Norland College[14] in the city of Bath. Norland was founded more than 125 years ago and would have been just the sort of place to have trained the fictional, magical Mary Poppins. Norland's aim has always been that a nanny should be a professional, trained in every aspect of childcare and development. That is also at the heart of Poppins's business model. A hindrance to the development of the nanny business has long been the near-impossibility of importing nannies from abroad: as was noted in Chapter 2, it is possible for foreign expatriates to get visas for this, but not for Japanese mothers. Changing that and allowing foreign nannies to be trained to professional standards would help to ease the pressure on working mothers and on daycare facilities. Politicians are strangely deaf to this idea, however. They often are deaf to new initiatives.

[14] http://www.norland.ac.uk.

6
Making a Political Impact

Koike Yuriko, Kuniya Hiroko, and Hayashi Fumiko

There is one measure of female participation in public life on which Japan has always scored among the lowest in the world. This is politics: the proportion of Diet members, prefectural governors or city mayors that are women. As of March 2019, only 13.8 per cent of Diet members (lower and upper houses combined)[1] were female, ranking Japan 165th among 193 countries, according to the Inter-Parliamentary Union. Among the forty-seven prefectural or metropolitan governors, only two were women at that date (Tokyo and Yamagata), and among Japan's 1,718 municipalities, only twenty-eight[2] had female mayors, or just 1.5 per cent. On many measures of gender equality Japan at least scores slightly better than South Korea, but not in politics. There, Japan is bottom of the class.

There are however pioneers trying to change this. That last statistic about female mayors was told to me[3] by one of the twenty-eight, namely Hayashi Fumiko, the mayor of Yokohama who in 2017 was elected to that post for a third term. Hayashi-san was the first female mayor of Yokohama when she won office in 2009, just as Koike Yuriko was later the first female governor of Tokyo when she won that office in 2016. Both Hayashi-san and Koike-san were already well used to being 'female firsts' during their previous careers, as first female chair of Nissan Auto Sales and Daiei

---

[1] *Nippon.com*, 8 March 2019. The figure for the House of Representatives at that date was 10.2 per cent, that for the House of Councillors 20.6 per cent.
[2] As of October 2017.
[3] Interview with Hayashi Fumiko, Official Residence of the Mayor of Yokohama, 5 October 2017.

Corporation in Hayashi-san's case, and first female defence minister in Koike-san's.

Meeting both of these quite formidable politicians, who are very different from one another in style and in their approaches to leadership, could risk making an outsider think that women might be about to surge to national prominence. Put Tokyo and Yokohama together, and you get roughly 40 per cent of Japan's annual GDP. But this would be misleading. While there are good reasons to be optimistic about the prospects for women's progress in companies and other organizations, rapid progress in politics looks harder to achieve.

In other countries, even ones that are quite conservative about gender equality, women have often made faster progress in politics than in other walks of life for the simple reason that in politics it is generally easier to jump over obstacles and rise on the basis of your personality, at much younger ages than in other fields. Young women often do particularly well. Selection in a democracy is, after all, about the person and their image rather than a strict set of skills or qualifications, and half the voters are female themselves. This does not mean that other countries have gender equality in politics: far from it. There has never been a female president of the United States nor of France, and there has never been a female prime minister of Italy, for example. Nevertheless, females have risen in those countries to many prominent political roles.

When I lived in Japan during part of the 1980s as a foreign correspondent the rise of Doi Takako to a leading role in the Japan Socialist Party, and even (in 1993) to be the first female speaker of the House of Representatives (Lower House of the Diet), gave the impression that something might be changing. But this was just as misleading as it would have been in Britain to conclude that gender equality was on its way just because Margaret Thatcher became the first female leader of the Conservative Party in 1975 and then our country's first female prime minister in 1979. Both Mrs Thatcher and Doi-san were exceptions, not evidence of a new rule. The Lower House elections of October 2017 confirmed this fact: the proportion of female Diet members remained at more or less the same dismally low level as in all elections since the first postwar votes in 1946. In response to that poor outcome, in May 2018 the Diet passed a law[4] calling upon political parties to 'equalize as much as possible' female and male candidates in national and local elections. But it was non-binding and so is unlikely to make much difference.

One place where women have been able to play an important political role is, however, in television programmes that are about government and current affairs, in which politicians are questioned and in which, as a result, political news can be made. When I went to interview Governor Koike at the Tokyo Metropolitan Government's headquarters, her opening comment to me when she came into the room was 'Emmott-san, do you remember when it was that you and I first met?'. I confess that I was not sure. Her answer was that we first met when she was working as an assistant on the Nippon TV talk show hosted by the famous interviewer Takemura Kenichi. Neither of us was exactly sure when this was, but it will have been during the 1980s as by 1985 she had herself become a TV anchor on business programmes at TV Tokyo before entering politics in 1992. At first she was a member of a small group called the Japan New Party, before joining the Liberal Democratic Party in 2002. Personally, I am the sort of journalist who would never have entered politics, because I would hate the public profile, the compromises, and the inevitable broken promises, and I suspect the same is true of another female anchorwoman who became famous for doing interviews about political subjects, Kuniya Hiroko.

As the host of NHK's *Close Up Gendai* programme ever since its launch in 1993, Kuniya-san interviewed all the great national and international political figures, along with many others, during her twenty-three years anchoring that show. But then in 2016 she lost her job for what seems to have been a very political reason: she told me[5] that her NHK bosses, seemingly pressured by senior people in

---

[4] https://www.japantimes.co.jp/news/2018/05/16/national/politics-diplomacy/diet-passes-nonbinding-legislation-aimed-increasing-women-politics/#.XhtPVS2ca9Q.
[5] Interview with Kuniya Hiroko, Imperial Hotel, Tokyo, 28 February 2017.

the Liberal Democratic Party and the team surrounding Prime Minister Abe, decided that her style of direct, well-informed, persistent questioning of politicians and senior officials was no longer appropriate.

Had she changed her style? Kuniya-san says she had not, and she is surely right. It was politics and in particular the politics of NHK management, that had changed. Public broadcasters always have to be careful to be fair and balanced in their coverage. But at the BBC in Britain or NHK in Japan, broadcasters have traditionally sought to do so by seeking to be balanced in their overall coverage: if some shows are critical of particular policies or points of view, the network must make sure that alternative positions and points of view get a chance to be aired in other prominent and well-watched shows. If every individual programme were forced to be balanced, then it would be impractical: an interview show like *Close Up Gendai* that ran a conversation with, for example, President Alberto Fujimori of Peru (as Kuniya-san did during his time in office in 1990–2000) that included points critical of him would then have to also find time for an interview with someone who praised him. In a show that lasts just twenty-six minutes each day, this would make for boring television that covered fewer subjects and would soon lose viewers.

The whole point of TV interviews of political figures is for the journalist concerned to ask direct, well-informed questions on behalf of the public. In other words, they should put the interviewee on the spot, not in an aggressive or partisan way but rather in an insistent, fair-minded pursuit of truthful answers and enlightenment for the viewer. The interviewer is asking questions on behalf of the public and in the public interest. That is very much what Kuniya-san became famous for on *Close Up Gendai*. By doing so, she had a real political impact, even without being herself a politician.

She is a disarmingly modest person. When she was forced out of her role at NHK, many people encouraged her to protest noisily in favour of journalistic independence and free speech. It is clear that political decisions, which she says began under Prime Minister Fukuda Yasuo in 2007–8, to appoint outsiders as NHK's director-general rather than insiders, are what explain the change in attitude to political talk-shows. Political influence on the nation's public broadcasting service was growing. But she says that when she was pushed out she didn't want to act as a martyr because 'it would risk causing trouble for all her old colleagues who were staying at NHK and trying to do their best.' The changes were not being decided by the programmers themselves, but by top management. So she chose to keep a low profile, especially during her first year after leaving.

Many journalists would have acted differently, making noisy comments about the threat to independent journalism and to public understanding of politics that was being posed by the interference of political parties and especially the prime minister's office. I rather think Koike-san would have acted in that way if something like that had happened to her while she was still a journalist: she wouldn't have taken it quietly. But everyone is different, and there were plenty of other people making a noise about the removal of Kuniya-san and some other prominent anchors on other shows at the same time. Rather than commenting about journalism and public broadcasting, Kuniya-san says she now wants to have an impact on people's understanding of sustainable development. That is an appropriate approach for a journalist to take: to act as an evangelist and public educator about an important issue, in newspapers and on TV.

There is no doubt that Kuniya-san has earned the right to speak out, through her decades of careful, impressive work. She won her first chance in television in New York in 1987 rather than at headquarters in Tokyo, unusually for someone in one of the big networks, as she was living there as a researcher and translator after having studied at Brown University on Rhode Island. She was also already 30 years old, so says 'I wasn't chosen for my pretty youth.' Business satellite channels were just being launched at that time, and Kuniya-san says modestly that she 'felt my Japanese wasn't really broadcast quality', but the producers at NHK said that this 'would be OK as no one was watching' at 3.00am Japanese time when her news programme was being broadcast.

NHK then asked her to move back to Japan as an anchor for international news, an opportunity which she grabbed but says it was a big failure. She had less than nine months experience and 'was quite naïve to think it could work'. Her inexperience showed, she says, and she lasted just half a year on that show before she was displaced and sent off to be a TV reporter on the road. But even from that role she was dropped after a year. It was clearly a tough introduction both to broadcasting and to professional life. But Kuniya-san thinks it was good for her: 'failure made me very determined to succeed' and 'made me more focused'.

Two things helped her climb back from these setbacks. One was a combination of support and constructive criticism from her husband, she says, who is a lawyer. 'The great thing about TV is that your partner really sees your work, so he literally saw me in disgrace.' The second thing was that that period—1989–93—was an extraordinary time for world news, with the Tiananmen massacre in Beijing, the fall of the Soviet Union and the Berlin Wall, the first Gulf war, and so much more. Producers and anchors with knowledge of world news were relatively scarce, which gave her the chance to do some quite intensive anchoring work for NHK, really learning the job. And it was at that point, in 1993, that NHK decided to launch *Close Up Gendai* as a daily political discussion show, and asked Kuniya-san to have a go at hosting it.

Japanese politics too was then going through big changes, with splits in the LDP and the election of the first non-LDP led government since 1955—headed by Hosokawa Morihiro, who coincidentally had invited Koike-san to join his Japan New Party and run for the House of Councillors—so NHK wanted the new show to be the main place in which it could highlight and explain what was going on. Hearing Kuniya-san describe the show's origins felt quite ironic given what happened to her more than two decades later, thanks to the changing political scene. She was the beneficiary of one change but later the victim of another.

Like politics, television is quite a rough place for women to work in, says Kuniya-san, because the hours are so long and the news so dominant that any idea of work-life balance has to be discarded. This makes it a very male environment, with all her bosses—the programme's chief editors—being men. Thinking back, Kuniya-san says that she thinks she 'was approved of because she accommodated male colleagues' ways, working late at night and agreeing to meetings on Sundays. I feel I was a bad role model for women.'

Most probably, she was a product of the times during which she was working. There was no real choice during the 1990s. But she cannot simply have been a follower, given her prominence and the leading position she attained. She told me that 'when you are working in a team, you should always ask yourself "what value can I add?"'. Her answer, she says, was to add value by the way in which she wrote and delivered her scripts: she was not just going to be an ornament reading out someone else's words. She rewrote scripts in her own way, insisting on having her colleagues check her work not mainly by reading the scripts but by listening to her rehearsal.

In fact, when writing her scripts she says 'I deliberately wrote them in hard-to-read writing so that they wouldn't just take the script away and rewrite it themselves.' That will have been quite a cunning way to be able to have her own impact, to keep control of her work in a domineering male environment. She leaned back as she spoke and laughed: 'I've never told anyone that before,' she said.

*   *   *

The Japanese political world has, for sure, been waiting to see how another former TV anchorwoman, Koike Yuriko, responds to her experience of failure during the 2017 Lower House elections: would it make her more determined or would it convince her she has risen as far as she can go? Ahead of those elections, she had for a time been the hottest political property in the country, even tipped to succeed Abe Shinzo as prime minister, whether by rejoining the LDP (she had left in May 2017 after having succeeded in winning the Tokyo Governorship against the party's opposition) or by sweeping the electoral board with her own new party. In July 2017 Koike-san's party, *Tomin First no Kai* (Tokyoites First) won a dramatic victory in the Tokyo Metropolitan Assembly elections in a daring coalition with the very party, *Komeito*,[6] that in national government is in

---

[6] *Komeito*, roughly translated as 'fair government party', is closely related to a major Buddhist religious organization, Soka Gakkai, and has been in coalition government with the LDP since 2012.

partnership with the LDP. To those analysts keen on speculation, it looked a precursor to luring *Komeito* to switch partners in due course at national level too. But 'in due course' never came: Prime Minister Abe chose to pre-empt any incursion into national politics by the popular Tokyo Governor by calling snap general elections for October.

With no time to prepare, Koike-san decided not to run in the national poll, claiming to want to do a proper job in Tokyo having only been elected the previous year. Her hastily cobbled-together national party, the strangely named 'Party of Hope' (*Kibo no To*), had to run without her as its standard-bearer and fared poorly. When what was previously the main opposition party, the Democratic Party of Japan, suddenly dissolved ahead of the elections, more or less offering itself to Koike-san on a plate, she and her party colleagues decided to rebuff the offer. An apparent opportunity was missed and instead a breakaway from the DPJ, calling itself the 'Constitutional Democratic Party of Japan', won more seats than Party of Hope.

As a result, having first[7] interviewed Governor Koike in early 2017 when her star was rising, I felt it necessary to request a second[8] interview with her to ask her about this political setback, which took place less than three months after the general elections and about a year after the first conversation. This request for a second interview was probably made easier by a very strict and somewhat annoying rule that she and her communications team at the Tokyo Metropolitan Government follow for interviews: they limit the interview to a maximum of twenty minutes, a time-limit which they enforce strictly. This is quite likely to be her own rule rather than that of the TMG staff, for it is very unusual for government bodies to impose limits as tight and universal as this. Whatever they may think of journalists, politicians do not generally go out of their way to annoy them (with the exception of course of Donald Trump). But perhaps being a former journalist herself, Koike-san

---

[7] Interview with Koike Yuriko, Tokyo Metropolitan Government offices, Shinjuku, Tokyo, 27 February 2017.
[8] Interview with Koike Yuriko, Tokyo Metropolitan Government offices, Shinjuku, Tokyo, 13 February 2018.

may have concluded that, in a sense, less is more: that keeping interviews short reduces risk and allows her to be able to put out her messages in an efficient way.

Both interviews were very friendly. But there was one key difference. In February 2017, although her staff had insisted that I come with an interpreter, Governor Koike decided to answer all my questions in English. Her English is not as perfect as Kuniya-san's, but then as a young woman she chose to study in Cairo to learn Arabic instead of going to the United States like her fellow broadcaster. Her English is nevertheless pretty good and she speaks very naturally in it. For my second interview, however, in February 2018, Governor Koike chose to respond mainly in Japanese. We were talking about politics and the aftermath of the elections, so she no doubt wanted to be precise and careful.

Her answers were quite sharp and striking. When I raised my first topic—her experience of the Lower House election—she immediately said, with a laugh, in English, 'I forgot.' 'How was the experience?', I reiterated. 'Oh, I enjoyed it,' she replied. But then she switched into Japanese and gave a more serious and careful answer. She and her Party of Hope had campaigned for only a limited time and yet it had still won almost 10 million votes in the proportional representation seats, she said. 'This showed how dissatisfied people are,' she said, with the present state of politics. But, she went on to admit, she had 'not been able to fulfil the initial goal of changing the way politics is in Japan'.

She said, with some emotion, that in Japan change comes far too slowly compared with other countries, with too many regulations, laws, and ordinances getting in the way. Moreover, she added, knowing the nature of my research, 'the roles played by women are not sufficient.' But clearly the impact of her party itself had been insufficient, and her response to the sudden dissolution of the Democratic Party of Japan when the election was announced proved to be maladroit.

Talk to virtually any political commentator and they will tell you that Koike-san is finished, that her political star is now in decline. Given that she is in charge of the immensely important Tokyo Metropolitan Government, will in due course host the Olympic

Games in her city, and that politics can change very quickly, this seems at best premature. The covid-19 pandemic in 2020 showed some signs of proving that point, since Koike-san, along with some other prominent governors, appeared more decisive, consistent and clear in their decision-making and communication about the crisis than was the case with Prime Minister Abe. His popularity declined while theirs—especially Koike-san and her equivalent in Osaka—rose. As this book went to press, she was due to run in Tokyo's gubernatorial elections on 5 July 2020 for a second term, and looked certain to win.

At that 2018 interview I asked her what she thought of her future in national politics and her answer was crisp and firm: 'I have no intention at all to run for national politics.' She emphasized that there are no national elections coming up and that she planned to concentrate on her job for Tokyo. What about after she has finished her term in Tokyo, I asked? 'I have no intention at all for national politics,' she repeated. But surely afterwards might be different, I said. 'I don't even know if I will be alive by then,' she joked. I pressed again. 'No means no,' she replied. Now, I wonder whether the pandemic might change that view, given that national elections are due by October 2021 at the latest.

Despite having ruled herself out of national politics, she was polite and interested enough to answer my next question, about her views about constitutional reform, given that this remains one of the biggest issues in national politics. Her response was broad and quite ambitious: she described the Japanese constitution as 'now like an ancient document, not a word of which has been changed. In the current constitution there is only a tiny stipulation about local government. We need to review the overall constitution,' she said, 'and change what needs to be changed.'

I naturally asked her views about Article Nine, the so-called pacifist clause that governs Japan's military. Her response was fairly clear: 'I have a question-mark over whether it is appropriate to include the Self Defence Forces at all in the constitution, which is above regular laws. The SDF is just one government entity.' In other words, she would like Article Nine to be abolished altogether. Other countries do not typically include references to their military forces in their constitutions. Free from direct responsibility in national politics, this modernizer (and former defence minister) is even more of an advocate of normalizing her country's constitution than are many of her former LDP colleagues.

In both of our interviews, I asked Governor Koike about the role of women and what could be done to facilitate a greater role. Her attitude was that things are improving but not rapidly enough: she quoted the fall of Japan in the World Economic Forum's Gender Equality Index as evidence that other countries are making more efforts than Japan and improving faster. Her emphasis was very much on the need to alter the male ways of working in corporations, ministries, and organizations such as the Tokyo Metropolitan Government. She told me she saw the problem clearly even when she was Minister of Defence in the first Abe government in 2007: 'the top graduates in the Defence Academy exams were always women. But later in their careers, men took over.'

Like Mayor Hayashi in Yokohama, Koike-san's Tokyo Metropolitan Government has been trying to put more money into daycare facilities so as to help women to stay at work. 'Today, the ratio of job-seekers in Tokyo is almost two applicants for every job,' she said; 'there is a tremendous labour shortage.' We are 'trying to ensure that 70,000 more babies have access to childcare' in Tokyo, which means that '70,000 more women are able to stay at work.' At the Tokyo Metropolitan Government, she says they are trying to promote changes in corporate work-styles by giving particular recognition to companies in which female workers are allowed to leave the workplace earlier in the evening and more flexibly in order to take care of family issues. With their own staff, they are even organizing *Konkatsu* matchmaking sessions to help boost marriage.

She acknowledged, however, that it is also desirable to help both men and women continue to work after they have reached their retirement age. 'The pension system is based on the old demographic pyramid,' she observed; 'it doesn't work any more.' By keeping on working, people can feel more attached to society. With a smile, she spoke with a kind of pity for retired men 'who feel that without their necktie and their business cards they have no identity'. It is better, she said, for them to be in work and have an identity.

For both of my interviews, quite a few officials from the Tokyo Metropolitan Government sat with us around the table. The same thing happened in the mayor's official residence in Yokohama when I interviewed Mayor Hayashi. There was a different feeling between these occasions, however, which my always observant interpreter pointed out to me afterwards. When Hayashi-san cited some data, someone among the officials often intervened, politely of course, to either correct or expand upon the information. When Koike-san cited some data, none of her officials said anything. The two leaders' styles are quite different: the feeling that Koike-san emanates is that she is the boss, and that the staff are just there to observe and take notes, not daring to speak up; with Hayashi-san the feeling is that this is more like a team, all of whom are encouraged to contribute. But they come from different backgrounds: while Koike-san made her name as a TV anchorwoman, which is a fairly (though not wholly) individualistic role, Hayashi-san had a long and successful career in business, managing teams of people.

*   *   *

For a business leader, Hayashi Fumiko is surprisingly quietly spoken. This[9] is a woman who so excelled in car sales that she became the top salesperson at Honda in 1977–87 and went on from there to work as a manager at BMW Japan from 1987–99, before becoming president of Volkswagen Japan in 1999, then chairman and CEO of Daiei Inc, the supermarket chain, in 2005, and later president of Nissan Auto Sales in 2008. Somehow, the stereotypical image of a champion salesperson, let alone a company president, is of some-one quite dominant, fast-talking, even loud. Not Hayashi-san. She has clearly been very oriented towards customers and towards teamwork, and now talks of the work of being a mayor as if it were a service business. No aggression or macho behaviour is in sight.

Such behaviour would anyway seem rather strange in the venue in which I met her. The official residence of the mayor of Yokohama is not a grand building but is very distinctive and historic, having been built in 1927 in a style reminiscent of both Art Deco and the

[9] https://www.city.yokohama.lg.jp/lang/residents/en/mayor/profile-en.html.

architecture of Frank Lloyd Wright, the American designer who was himself highly influenced by Japanese design. The residence is on a fairly small site by comparison with the sort of houses that major cities have often built for their mayors, but it has a charming garden with a nice view across the city. I see a set of binoculars next to a chair by the window and am told that Mayor Hayashi likes to use them to watch the birds in the garden. The woman who then enters the meeting room is small, smiling, and unassuming.

Her biggest and most noticeable achievement during her first two terms as mayor after she was first elected in 2009 was to drive the city of Yokohama to entirely eliminate waiting lists for childcare for babies. In this regard, the city is the envy of Tokyo next door and of many others. At first, says Mayor Hayashi, city officials were reluctant to accept a zero-waiting-list target, arguing that it was unachievable because if the supply of daycare increases, so will the demand, meaning that they would be chasing an elusive and ever-moving target. Hayashi-san, accustomed to working to targets in the car sales business, insisted and eventually got her way.

Since our conversation began with childcare, I asked Hayashi-san what else was on her agenda for improving the role of women in work and in society? She cited three main items. First, she said, women 'need role models, which are hard to find'. So Yokohama has organized a series of conferences to showcase successful female professionals and to encourage women to build up their networks of associates.

Second, the city has been 'nurturing female entrepreneurs' by providing shared office space for start-ups with consultants available to give advice, by offering low interest loans, and by providing facilities in which entrepreneurs can test their ideas and even models of their products. She said that the city knows of '221 female entrepreneurs who have started businesses over a six-year period', helped by this encouragement. The city recently made a survey of these companies and found that 80 per cent were still in business.

Finally she said approvingly that many companies in the city are now providing training to their staff in managing and fostering diversity. She was elected for a competing political party (the then Democratic Party of Japan) but nevertheless speaks positively about the efforts that have been made by Prime Minister Abe's administration since 2012 to promote women in the workforce. Her own philosophy of management accords in particular with the Abe government's effort to encourage reforms in work-style for both women and men, and to discourage overtime.

Hayashi-san went to work straight from high school in 1965: she did not attend either junior college or university. At first, she hopped between jobs as an assistant to various men, at Toray Industries, Matsushita Electric Industrial (Panasonic) and others, before joining Honda Auto Yokohama in 1977. There she amazed her male colleagues by becoming the firm's top salesperson by the end of her first year. She had met her husband while working at Panasonic, and they had a daughter. When she was later offered the job as president of BMW Japan she asked his opinion, unsure whether she felt up to it. 'Take it,' he said. 'Why not?'

Was there any real work-life balance in the auto industry in those days, I asked? Not at all, she said. When she became a manager, 'I came to decide that it really all depends on the leader. So when I became the leader I organized things so as to be able to leave the office early, so as to set an example.' As a manager and later a company president, she says she 'constantly reminded employees that they really didn't have to work too hard, doing unnecessary work such as overtime'. I told them 'go home early.'

She has continued this trait at Yokohama City Government: 'I tell people who are working overtime "this is not your house—you cannot use the chairs and electricity without permission".' Her impression is that these work-style issues have become much better compared with the 1960s and 1970s for non-managerial women, who can now 'take on jobs that are flexible enough to suit their lifestyles' but the issue 'has not been resolved for managerial women'. The pressure to work overtime remains a big problem, in her view.

She believes that managers need to achieve a greater level of empathy and understanding between them and employees, and that being empathetic remains 'too uncommon'. I asked whether there are Japanese executives she admires who have this trait. Her immediate answer was Inamori Kazuo, the founder of Kyocera and later chairman of Japan Air Lines. She said that for a long time

'I had a book written by him next to my pillow. Whenever I encountered troubles I would go back and read it again.' She said she was particularly impressed by a press conference he gave when he took over as chairman of the bankrupt Japan Air Lines in 2010 and said 'he took on the job not to restructure the company but rather to make the employees happy again.' It sounds a bit sentimental. But what she calls 'people-centric management' is her common theme: that happy employees are more productive and work harder, that empathy is necessary to achieve this, and that one of the hardest things for a manager to learn is how to give praise and encouragement to staff.

Hayashi-san believes, in fact, that women are 'better than men at acceptance and empathy, and are better at standing alongside others. These traits are very important for management. That is why I think it is important that more women hold top positions.' It is also, she says, very important 'that managers should show their weak points to staff members. I show my weak points. This helps staff support bosses,' she says, and promotes more empathy. And in politics too? Is it right to show your weaknesses in politics?

Mayor Hayashi, unusually, dodges the question a little by saying that municipalities are different from other levels of politics because those in city government are much closer to the people, delivering services and executing some of the policies of central government too. You cannot, she says, 'conceal anything from citizens'. I think I have met plenty of mayors who have done just that, but I concede the point. This is not someone to have an argument with. Mayor Hayashi is just too positive and empathetic for that.

7
Creating Art, Interpreting Life

Shinoda Toko, Nishimoto Tomomi, and Kawase Naomi

The field research for this book began in the spring of 2016 when I went to visit, and interview,[1] the then 103-year-old artist, Shinoda Toko, in the studio in Aoyama in Tokyo where she has lived and worked for more than seventy years. As this seemingly frail woman, who in my eyes resembled a thin bird dressed in a kimono, showed me the huge ink-stone that she bought from a shop in Kanda in Tokyo in the 1940s and has used ever since, I understood that one of the vital things about her art is its physicality. I suspect that the physical connection she makes with her brushes, ink, and paint on a daily basis is almost more important to her life and her art than what she is thinking and perhaps even than what she is feeling. Many months later, as I watched the then 48-year-old orchestra conductor, Nishimoto Tomomi, in her third rehearsal of the day, I had a similar sensation. Her physical exertion, her display of energy, her bodily involvement all play a central role in her music. After just sitting watching her and the orchestra I felt I needed to take a shower.

Shinoda-san's art began as abstract, *sumi-e*[2] calligraphy but in the eight decades since her first solo exhibition took place in Tokyo in 1940 it has evolved into far more abstract forms although still often involving a strong calligraphic element[3]. Among her art the most memorable example I have seen has to be her 100-foot-long mural

---

[1] Interview with Shinoda Toko, Aoyama, Tokyo, 12 April 2016.

[2] *Sumi-e* means black ink painting. Common across East Asia, it originated in China during the Tang dynasty (618–907 AD).

[3] https://www.tokyoweekender.com/2019/03/5-things-might-not-know-toko-shinoda/

at the Zojoji temple next to Shiba Park in Tokyo which consists of huge calligraphic black-ink shapes interspersed with white space, which she painted in 1974. She became internationally known during the 1950s when the art form known as Abstract Expressionism came into vogue in New York, led by such artists as Jackson Pollock and Mark Rothko, and some of her work was exhibited at the Museum of Modern Art. She had gone to spend about two years in New York in 1956–8, renewing her visa every two months and finding her way ingeniously past restrictions on access to the foreign currency that any Japanese needed if they were to finance such a trip. That, as it happens, was the year when I was born, so I needed no other proof of the difference in our ages and eras than when she spoke about the New York of 1956. 'I thought America was a great country, just for the fact that so many top galleries could be owned by women,' she said. Her own paintings were taken up by one of the main dealerships promoting Abstract Expressionism, the Betty Parsons Gallery.

*   *   *

Calligraphy is a particularly physical art form, dealing as it does in the immediate impact of brush and ink on to paper, and so in the direct transmission of feelings by the artist to the art and ultimately to its viewers. Orchestral conducting, Nishimoto-san told[4] me, is similarly about the transmission of passions and of feelings through physical actions. Unlike with painting or calligraphy, of course, such orchestral performance is almost always of music that someone else has written. Yet even then the important part lies in the difference that particular conductors and musicians make to the performances. 'I think the job of an artist is to add my words to that tune, like adding my blood, my flesh, recreating the work to make it my work,' Nishimoto-san said. She first felt she was really achieving what she wanted to, she said, when in her mid-30s she found that audiences were truly sensing 'that my performances reflected my bitter experiences'. 'It was a kind of a breakthrough,' she said.

---

[4] Interview with Nishimoto Tomomi, Suginami Public Hall, Ogikubo, Tokyo, 13 July 2017.

Seeing this successful, popular woman, looking to be in her absolute element in a Tokyo concert hall surrounded by the orchestra, I wondered what sort of bitterness she could possibly harbour? As she answered, it was clear that in some ways she has had to struggle to achieve what she has. This was despite coming from quite a musical family—her mother was a vocalist, her aunt plays the piano and the organ, and among her relatives were five people who had graduated at one time or other from music college. Nishimoto-san too went to music college after graduating from high school, but then at the age of 26 decided she should go to St Petersburg, in Russia, to study to be a conductor. No one in her family would help to finance her study abroad, so she had to raise the funds on her own. While at music college she worked as an assistant to an opera director, ultimately saving up the $10,000 she needed to pay the St Petersburg fees and living costs for one year. After that year, she moved to and fro between Japan and St Petersburg, returning home each time to earn and save up the money to be able to go back for periods of study.

While Shinoda-san found inspiration in America and in the freedoms adopted by artists there, Nishimoto-san found her inspiration in Russian teachers and conductors. She says she felt even as a child that with Russian pianists, violinists, cellists, and other musicians, 'although they were playing their instruments, they were actually talking through their music.' She cites her teacher in St Petersburg, Ilya Mushin, as a special influence because he was very passionate in his conducting, even at the age of 94.

In truth, as a successful female orchestra conductor Nishimoto-san is unusual all over the world, not just in Japan. This remains a predominantly male profession, globally. She says that her teacher Ilya Mushin 'used to say that it was far more difficult for a woman to be a conductor than to be a lieutenant in the Russian army', as the role is physically demanding. Someone with a weak and soft voice and quite a small appearance would find it difficult to have an impact. But as Nishimoto-san said, although physical impact is necessary, what is most needed 'is mental energy, mental strength'. She is fortunately quite tall, which probably helps, and she has done physical training so as to gain stamina. She says conducting puts particular burdens on to her neck, which I can imagine as I watch the rehearsal and see her head moving violently, her hair flying from side to side. But she nevertheless says that now that she is able to build more immediate trust with the players, she doesn't need to exaggerate her movements as much as in the past.

Another source of the bitterness that she says is reflected in her performances is the difficulty she encountered at first by virtue of being a conductor who was younger than many of the players in her orchestras. 'In Japan it is always hard to be in a leadership position as a younger person and as a woman....I felt that as well as a glass ceiling there were also glass walls all around me,' she added. 'But I don't feel there are glass walls around me any more.'

Nonetheless, she is clearly sensitive about some of the things music critics have written about her, especially in the early days when she was making her reputation. 'At first rumours were spread for example that I had paid a bribe to win something, but this was not true at all.' Reading about it, I think plenty of even nastier rumours were spread, but that is unfortunately not unusual in male-dominated societies when women achieve success. Nishimoto-san places it in a particular Japanese context: 'I am the one among musical people who came from a totally different course from the path normally followed by graduates from music school. There had been no such example like me, so people asked why and how this could have happened,' she said. And she added ruefully something that Mayor Hayashi also pointed out: 'In Japan when one does something that is unprecedented people don't react well.'

Nishimoto-san is now well known in other Asian countries, including Taiwan and China, and performs regularly at the Vatican in Rome. The Vatican performances originated from the fact that although her own family are not Catholics, some of her relatives came from Ikitsuki Island near Nagasaki in Kyushu in south-west Japan, which was one of the main centres of 'Hidden Christians'[5] in the seventeenth and eighteenth centuries. When she was first

---

[5] Known as *Kakure Kirishitan* in Japanese, Hidden Christians were people who continued to practise their faith during the period when Christianity was banned in Japan, from 1614 to 1873. As Jesuit missionaries had previously landed and made conversions mainly in the Nagasaki area, most Hidden Christians were there: http://kirishitan.jp/values_en/val002.

invited to perform at the Vatican, she suggested that a chant by Francis Xavier, the Jesuit missionary, which had remained in use on Ikitsuki island as part of local culture should form part of her repertoire at the Vatican. 'One thing I feel is that history is always told from the winners' side. Always the people who lost are perished and their voices are lost. But in local culture they are preserved, and I feel a mission to restore those things.'

She mentioned another historical project which took my mind also back to Shinoda-san, albeit tangentially. Nishimoto-san said that in the autumn of 2017 she was going to be conducting a performance of the musical Noh play Sotoba Komachi and was not just conducting but also arranging the music and acting as art director. In this play, a very old woman is found sitting on a Buddhist gravepost, a wooden stupa. She is Ono no Komachi, one of the great poets of the Heian Period[6] and who was said to have been a beauty in her youth. Now 100 years old in the play, as she is sitting on the ruined stupa two priests come across her and tell her she must get off the stupa and show it more respect.

In hearing and reading about this story, I thought of Shinoda Toko not merely because like Ono no Komachi she is over 100 years old. It was something she said. I asked her whether she teaches others and whether there are artists and architects who she admires. Her answer to the first question was dismissive: she doesn't take apprentices or teach anybody because 'art is individual. It is not something I can teach.' And to the second question her answer was also somewhat quirky, perhaps even rather critical, in a way that could even have come from the mouth of Ono no Komachi, in the parts of the play when she is being confident and poetic. Shinoda-san answered my question about whether she admired the architect Tange Kenzo, by saying, yes, she had met him a few times. But, she added, 'I think people who admire are people who want to be admired by others. I respect people who do not want to be respected.'

*   *   *

---

[6] 794–1185 A D.

Kawase Naomi was somewhat gentler in her responses to my questions when I met[7] the film director in her production company's office in Nara. But I still suspect that she might agree with Shinoda-san's point, or at least she acts as if she does. Her films are not the work of someone who is trying to be popular, or liked, or even admired, although she often is in fact admired, especially in film festivals such as the one held every year in Cannes in France, where she has won prizes. Shinoda-san said to me 'I did all my work in the way I wanted,' and I think Kawase-san would say something very similar.

At the time I met her, in July 2017, she was preparing for an unusual role, as director of a production of Giacomo Puccini's famous opera Tosca. This was to be the first time she had directed in a theatre. But there was to be something else innovative about this production. In Puccini's original, Tosca ends in tragedy, with all the main characters dying, including the heroine, Floria Tosca. Kawase-san's production, however, was to end differently, I was told: she was adapting it to have a more hopeful, less tragic ending. She was doing her work in the way she wanted. Whether or not Puccini would have approved must remain a matter for speculation. But in 2019 it was announced that she had been commissioned to direct the official film of the 2020 Olympic and Paralympic Games in Tokyo, which seemed sure to have a hopeful, aspirational flavour.

In film, she says, 'the most important thing is to have one's own originality and strength. Unless you have a strong belief that "I have just got to film this" you cannot stand out.' Her films are not easy to watch nor, in some respects, are they easy to understand. Making things easy is not her intention or interest. By making the central character of An ['Sweet Bean', 2015] a victim of Hansen's disease (i.e. leprosy), or the main character of Hikari ['Radiance', 2017] someone who is going blind, she is not seeking to make audiences feel comfortable or happy. Rather, she seems to want to explore and portray the difficult and complex relationships that people have with each other. Family is a recurrent theme in her films, but her families are generally not either happy or united, but rather are

---

[7] Interview with Kawase Naomi, Kumie Productions Head Office, Nara, 6 July 2017.

broken or else breaking up, which reflects her own experience as a child. Her parents split up early in her childhood, and she was raised in rural Nara by her great-aunt. She divorced from her own husband after less than three years of marriage. She has a young son, who in fact came into the production company office while I was there, and who she is raising as a single mother.

I asked her what was her measure of success? 'For me', she replied, 'success means to be able to stay calm, to be able to meet people, and to create something new.' Knowing that many of her films find fairly small audiences—*An* has won her biggest audience so far—she says with gratitude that 'still there are people who want to finance the kind of films I want to make.' 'An interesting thing I have noticed is that more people who have made a success in business want to invest in me and in other directors who might win prizes in Cannes and so get fame through my works.' I can see that although films are not at all cheap to make—the budget for *Hikari* was $1.5 million, Kawase san told me, which is nonetheless at the cheaper end of feature-film making—for those businesspeople who have made a lot of money, an investment in such a film can represent a relatively economical way to gain an association with fame and with art.

Such investors will have been encouraged by learning of Kawase-san's first full feature film, *Moe no Suzaku*, which in 1997 won the 'Camera d'Or' prize in Cannes for the best new film, a prize of which she was the youngest ever winner (at the age then of 28). She had previously made documentaries, and a cameraman who saw a showing of a private documentary she had made in 1992 introduced her to the WoWoW satellite and pay-per-view TV company which was keen on backing some original, independent films. That private documentary, called *Ni tsutsumarete* ('Embracing'), was about her search for her father, which was 'very important to me personally'. She made it while working as a lecturer at the Osaka School of Photography, where she had studied film as an undergraduate.

When she started filming *Moe no Suzaku*, which tells the story of the dissolution of a rural family, she was just 26 years old. By her account, the team that was making the film almost dissolved too, partway through the filming. She says she felt very isolated, amid a cast and crew who were mainly male and mostly older, and who 'felt I was very young and inexperienced'. Suddenly, some of the cast became so frustrated with her that they threatened to leave, including the main actor, Kunimura Jun, who was at that time the only professional in the cast. 'I was determined to carry on. Even if I could only use 8mm film [rather than professional 35mm] I was going to finish it. The producer from WoWoW asked me whether I really wanted to continue. I said yes. So he then persuaded the cast and crew to stay.' Perhaps, she says with hindsight, it was fortunate that the WoWoW producer was not so much older than her, was from TV, and worked for a company that was committed to doing something new and outside their usual TV world. 'If I had said I might quit, then that would have been the end.'

'Women', says Kawase-san, 'have to stay tougher as directors. Overcoming difficulties makes you stronger.' It is a familiar refrain, but it is also true that as for orchestra conductors it is relatively rare for women to have successful careers as film directors. As she told me, 'artists and actors can be quite self-contained, but directors have to have more strength so as to supervise a crew and cast as well as to maintain a schedule.' She certainly also thinks that female directors suffer discrimination: 'I recently heard that the guarantees that female directors are receiving are only 50% of those received by men,' and by this she meant worldwide. By 'guarantee' she was referring to the system of payment in the film industry under which directors get paid a fixed amount as a guarantee, and then on top of that receive a share of income if it surpasses a certain level.

Naturally, she speaks about discrimination against women with strong feelings and emotions. I asked her whether she would find the story of women's place in society interesting enough to film. Her response was candid and straightforward: 'That is not something I am aiming at, as it may require energy that I don't want to use.' She felt, she said, that if she were to focus on women struggling to succeed in work or society she might 'be seen as an activist or political' and she doesn't want that. She says that 'it is OK if my films have some impact on society. But I don't want a secondary role as an activist.'

*　　*　　*

Shinoda Toko, with whom we began this chapter, has certainly seen a lot of battles during her life, though she has clearly always chosen to focus on her art rather than on what was going on around her. Born in Dalian in China in 1913, in the area that Japan controlled following the Russo-Japanese war of 1904/5, she grew up mainly in Gifu prefecture as her family soon moved back to Japan from China. She told me 'I never thought to become an artist when I was young. I just became one.' Her oldest memory of art is as a student in art class at age 14 or 15, when she was asked to draw anything she liked, chose a plant, but opted to draw the leaves rather than the whole flower. She says her teacher said that her style was rather like French 'secessionist' art, which she says started her thinking about art.

Shinoda-san's parents told her she should get married. But 'I wanted my own way, and to live on my own. I couldn't get married, I was timid and did not want to go to a stranger's house.' So instead she took a job as a calligraphy teacher to earn a living. 'I started to teach in a very free way, encouraging my pupils to make their own characters. That is the first time when I felt I was different. I didn't want to emulate or imitate other people.' Then war broke out and, as she said, 'art became obscure.' But still she put on an exhibition at Kyukyodo gallery in Ginza in central Tokyo, her first solo showing. I asked whether that exhibition was successful. 'There were some reviews in art newspapers who said mine was a self-taught style. Others described my work as "brilliant, with excellent touches". But others said I was derailed from the long history of calligraphy. This was true, as I did not follow tradition.'

Not following tradition: that seems a good summary of Shinoda-san's approach to life. As mentioned before, her stay in New York in 1956–8 played an important role and she sold some of her works to John D. Rockefeller and his wife, who were employing curators to build their collection. But she nevertheless returned to Japan and stayed home ever since. 'I felt Japanese society did change after the war, liberating women to a certain extent. A woman could establish herself on her own, if she had the will.' I asked her what she thought of young Japanese women today, but she refused to answer: 'I am not interested in other people, so I couldn't have been a critic. I do not observe. I am a person who creates. I am indifferent to other people.'

As we finished our formal conversation, Shinoda-san invited me to stay for tea. This was served by her (then) 78-year-old assistant, Imamura-san, who at that time came to look after her on six days a week, travelling an hour each way to do so, having worked for Shinoda-san for about fifty years. As a symbol of the demography of modern Japan, there couldn't have been a better example.

I don't however think Shinoda-san would want to think of herself as an 'example' of anything:

> I have never regarded myself as an artist. I have always just wanted to make something as a form, but I never know what kind of force made me produce this art. A person is mysterious. For everyone what is beautiful is different. I still don't have an answer to what 'art' is after one hundred years. Food, yes; language yes; but art—I don't know if art is really important to a human being and what it really is. And I have never given a thought to whether art is a man's world or a woman's world. It is a job.

8
Representing Japan, Defending Human Rights

Miyoshi Mari and Osa Yukie

I did not expect to be handed a gift when I finished my interview[1] at the Japanese embassy in Dublin, and if I was to be given a gift I certainly would not have expected to be handed a biography of a former Irish prisoner of war. But then the Japanese Ambassador Extraordinary and Plenipotentiary to the Republic of Ireland, to give the role its full name, is not a standard-issue diplomat. For a start, as will be obvious from the fact that she is being featured in this book, Miyoshi Mari is a woman. She is currently one of the most senior females in the Ministry of Foreign Affairs (*Gaimusho* in Japanese), having attained director-general level in 2014 before she was posted to Ireland in 2016 for a three-year posting. When she returned to Tokyo in August 2019 she was given the impressively broad job of overseeing 'International Cooperation for Countering Terrorism and International Organized Crime and Arctic Affairs'.

The book[2] Ambassador Miyoshi handed me in Dublin was called *The Doctor's Sword*, and it told the fascinating but often troubling story of the life of Aidan MacCarthy. He was a doctor from Cork on the south coast of Ireland who was stationed in Sumatra in Indonesia by the British Royal Air Force and taken prisoner by the Japanese Imperial Army in 1942 when that army occupied the country. He was sent to Japan in 1944 to work and was held

---

[1] Interview with Miyoshi Mari, Embassy of Japan, Dublin, 19 September 2017.
[2] Bob Jackson, *A Doctor's Sword* (The Collins Press, 2017).

prisoner in Nagasaki where, fortunately, he survived the atomic bomb that was dropped on the city by the United States on 9 August 1945. When the surrender took place and prisoners were freed, Dr MacCarthy took command of his camp and in effect saved the Japanese commander from being attacked and potentially killed by the other prisoners. In gratitude, the commander, Second Lieutenant Kusuno Isao, handed Dr MacCarthy his ceremonial sword. Following Dr MacCarthy's return to Ireland, that sword was put on display in the family's bar in Cork.

It is a remarkable story. To an Englishman, one of the first things that is remarkable about it is that this heroic doctor in the Royal Air Force was Irish, for his country was by then independent from the United Kingdom (since 1921) and officially took a neutral stance during the second world war. Relations between our two countries at that time (and at several times since) were rather bitter and tense. So why would an Irishman join the armed forces of the country's former colonial occupier and oppressor? The reason is that despite our political differences, the human connections between our countries remained close. Like many of his countrymen in the 1930s, Dr MacCarthy moved to England to find work and then when war came he volunteered to join the RAF as a doctor. It is estimated that about 50,000–60,000 Irish citizens fought in the British armed forces during the second world war.

The second remarkable thing about Dr MacCarthy's story is how he survived a series of horrific experiences and terrible treatment in the prisoner-of-war camps in Indonesia and Japan, thanks to a lot of luck and also probably to his medical knowledge and his character. Yet he still retained a strong sense of humanity and spirit of reconciliation, the result of which was his protection of Second Lieutenant Kusuno. That is also what explains the third remarkable thing—the fact that a Japanese ambassador gave me a book that is full of stories of appalling behaviour in her country's prison camps. Quite rightly, the message that mattered to her, and that she wished to reinforce, was one of reconciliation.

In a simplistic sense, you might say that diplomacy is always about reconciliation. It is about finding agreement between countries on issues of mutual concern. But it is also about representing your country and pursuing and defending its interests. A lot of ambassadors, whether from Japan or from other countries, tend to respond to political pressure on their home governments by emphasizing the defence of national interests and the representation of official political stances, more than reconciliation. When discussion turns to the history of the Sino-Japanese war or the second world war, Japanese diplomats typically (and understandably) try to say as little as possible or, in a few cases, take a rather defensive position. They do not hand out books detailing the horrific side of war from the perspective of Japan's former opponents. Personally, I think they should, if they accompany such recognition with an embrace of common interests in understanding the past and finding ways to avoid any repetition, by our countries or by others.

Well before she had given me this welcome gift, I asked Ambassador Miyoshi why, when she graduated (as an unusual female student in those days) from the University of Tokyo's law department, she had applied to join the Ministry of Foreign Affairs, where she was the only female recruit to the diplomatic corps in 1980. She could no doubt have sought to join all sorts of other ministries, if a career in government was what she sought.

With hindsight, her answer helped also to explain her interest in the book about Dr MacCarthy. It was that one of her grandfathers had been killed in 1937 in battle in Shanghai during the Sino-Japanese war. Her mother, who was born in 1938, never saw her father. In her family, young Mari was always told about 'the misery of war', she said. When she grew up, she decided that the sort of job where she might be able to do most to work for peace and reconciliation was one in diplomacy.

She was among Japan's earliest female diplomats. The Ministry of Foreign Affairs had employed a small handful of women during the 1950s but began to recruit women as diplomats as a routine matter of policy only in 1978. The first ever female ambassador was Takahashi Nobuko, who was seconded by the Ministry of Labour and was made ambassador to Denmark in 1980. Two women were admitted as new recruits in each of 1978 and 1979, and then in Ambassador Miyoshi's year she says she was just one woman alongside twenty-eight male recruits; in 1981, three were admitted.

In 2016, however, there were ten women among the twenty-eight new recruits. Among recruits for non-diplomatic roles, she says the balance between men and women is now about 50-50. In the future, even if some leave for family reasons or to take up alternative careers, there will be an increasing supply of potential female ambassadors and directors-general. There are now only about ten female ambassadors in all (I say 'about' because the number naturally keeps changing as postings begin and end all the time), but the number is sure to rise.

It hasn't been an easy career, but Miyoshi-san evidently enjoys it thoroughly and said she has found her thirty-seven years (as of 2017) in the ministry pretty satisfying. She has spent seventeen of those thirty-seven years abroad, in foreign postings, at first as part of the 'German school' of the ministry with a spell at the embassy to Austria. When she returned from Vienna in 1985 she got married to a friend from the University of Tokyo who worked in the Ministry for the Environment, and they had a daughter in 1990. Her maternity leave lasted six weeks before the birth and then just eight weeks afterwards, which she told me was standard policy then in all the ministries. Once she returned to work, her baby daughter lived principally with Miyoshi-san's mother in Kamakura.

Miyoshi-san's job when she returned from giving birth was in the ministry's Protocol Office, responsible for handling important visitors at the time such as Mikhail Gorbachev, the Secretary-General of the Soviet Communist Party, and President George H. W. Bush. Protocol work was quite suitable for a young mother because compared with other diplomatic roles it was less vulnerable to being affected by news or negotiations, for which staff would often have to work late nights and at weekends, at short notice.

Then, in any case, the family had what could be described either as a lucky break or a case of far-sighted, flexible human resources planning by the ministry. In 1992 Miyoshi-san's husband was posted by his ministry to work in Geneva, in Switzerland, so she also asked for an assignment there at Japan's Permanent Mission to the International Organisations, which means Japan's embassy to the various branches of the United Nations that are located in Switzerland. Fortunately, the request was granted. She and her husband were therefore able to go together to Geneva with their daughter and a babysitter, meaning that during her formative years their daughter was there with them as a family, in a city and in circumstances that must count as quite ideal for raising a young child.

That posting also meant that Miyoshi-san was able to work closely with the woman that I think of as having been, during all my time writing about Japan, the country's first real de facto global female ambassador: Ogata Sadako,[3] who was the UN High Commissioner for Refugees for nine years from 1991–2000. It was a time when refugees were big news and a massive worldwide concern, especially thanks to the war in the countries of the former Yugoslavia, and African wars and civil wars in Rwanda and Congo, so Ogata-san was in a very hot seat and had true global recognition. She was never formally a member of Japan's Ministry of Foreign Affairs— and reportedly turned down an offer from the Koizumi administration to become foreign minister in 2002, following Tanaka Makiko's resignation from that role.

When she returned from the Geneva posting in 1995, Miyoshi-san joined the ministry's Economic Co-Operation Bureau, dealing with overseas aid, which was also often connected to refugee crises and humanitarian disasters, and then became involved in the negotiations for the Kyoto Protocol on climate change in 1997. I could sense, as Miyoshi-san spoke about these roles and the challenges she had to deal with, a feeling of excitement at being a witness to important events and issues, and a sense of the quite heavy responsibility of trying to deal with them.

Such events and negotiations rarely happen simply in day-time working hours, especially as they are occurring in every time zone around the globe. Thus work-life balance cannot have been easy. Miyoshi-san answered that this was one way in which the working practices of the ministry had changed a great deal during her career. 'When I entered the ministry, we had to work on Saturdays and although we officially had twenty days holiday every year we couldn't use it. Nowadays we can take those holidays, and working

---

[3] Ogata Sadako, 1927–2019: https://www.japantimes.co.jp/news/2019/10/29/national/sadako-ogata-dies/#.XhxYTi2ca9Q.

conditions are better.' She recalled how, in 1985 just two weeks before her wedding, she took part in a mission with Prime Minister Nakasone Yasuhiro to the G7 meeting of the top industrialized countries in Bonn, Germany, and then shortly after the wedding had to work in the team supporting a visit to Japan by France's President Francois Mitterrand. Faced with overnight work, the team had to resort to sleeping in their director-general's office. 'Now, a room and shower have been provided. Working conditions today have improved a lot since my early years at the Foreign Ministry.'

Bringing up a daughter while doing diplomatic work depended on a lot of support from Miyoshi-san's mother. After the family returned to Japan in 1995 they divided their lives between Kamakura, where her parents and daughter stayed, and Yokohama, where she and her husband lived. Miyoshi-san shuttled between the two. At the age of 9, when Miyoshi-san was given a posting to be a senior diplomat in the Japanese embassy in Germany, her daughter decided she preferred to stay in Japan with her father and her schoolfriends, rather than move to Berlin with her mother. At the time of our interview the daughter was 27 years old and working in Yokohama on the preparation for the Olympic Games. I asked Miyoshi-san whether she thought her daughter would choose to have a family or not. 'I think she would like a family but would also like to continue her work, so probably I will look after our grandchildren,' she said with a smile.

It is perhaps a little unfair to ask someone who has devoted their life to international affairs and has often lived abroad what she thinks of young Japanese women today. But I asked Miyoshi-san anyway, since she had been speaking about her daughter. Apart from her daughter, she answered that 'I feel Japanese girls have become too conservative, they like to stay in one place.' She fears, in fact, that this is true of young Japanese in general, both male and female, who have in her view become 'less open-minded and adventurous'. That is why, as she said, it is now fairly rare to find Japanese students at Harvard University, which, like other top universities around the world, is full of Chinese students. Nevertheless, in her then home town of Dublin, she told me with delight, there are five hundred Japanese students enrolled at Dublin City University, which has a strong English-language programme. Perhaps some of them, female or male, will think of following in Ambassador Miyoshi's footsteps.

*   *   *

Osa Yukie is another woman who has spent a lot of time abroad, in quite surprising places. She is not a diplomat but is an academic who has specialized in the study of war crimes and of post-war reconciliation and justice, and is now also president of the Association for Aid and Relief Japan (AAR), a non-profit dedicated to helping refugees fleeing conflict and persecution. AAR was set up by a female campaigner, Sohma Yukika, in 1979, in response to the issue then of how to help refugees from Vietnam and other parts of Indo-China.

We met[4] in Osa-san's office at Rikkyo University in November 2017 just one week after the verdict had been announced in the trial of Ratko Mladic for genocide, war crimes, and crimes against humanity at the United Nations-backed International Criminal Tribunal for the former Yugoslavia (ICTY). General Mladic was nicknamed 'the butcher of Bosnia' during the terrible civil wars in 1991–5 that took place after the break-up of the state of Yugoslavia into its former constituent countries of Bosnia, Serbia, Montenegro, Croatia, and others. After the main part of the war ended with a peace agreement in Dayton, Ohio, drawn up by the United States, the ICTY began to investigate and put on trial people accused of war crimes. In 2011, the by then former General Mladic was captured after a long period as a fugitive and put on trial in The Hague. To my surprise and great interest, Osa-san remarked, almost casually, that during the 1990s war she had known General Mladic personally.

In fact, Osa-san wrote her PhD thesis on Srebrenica, the town in Bosnia that was the scene of one of the Yugoslav wars' most terrible massacres. In July 1995 more than eight thousand Bosnian Muslim men and boys were killed by the army under General Mladic's command. A force of Dutch UN peacekeepers were present to protect the town, but proved unable to prevent the killings. Osa-san was

---

[4] Interview with Osa Yukie, Rikkyo University, Tokyo, 30 November 2017.

working for AAR at that time and was sent to former Yugoslavia by the non-profit. As she put it quite dispassionately, she became 'a specialist on genocide and on transitional justice', thanks to this experience.

A decade and a half later with the trials and investigations proceeding, Osa-san felt compelled to return to the subject of General Mladic, genocide, and transitional justice. She obtained a grant from the Ministry of Education to finance two research trips to The Hague to follow the ICTY trials, and in particular that of General Mladic. 'I wanted to be there personally, because I had met him.' As she said, she feels that in the process of justice and reconciliation that has been going on following the Yugoslav wars, 'there is a strong parallel to post-war Japan', with the Tokyo trials of 1946–8. In the case of Srebrenica, by 2017 it was already twenty-two years after the massacre and she felt there had been no reconciliation and many war criminals still free. To her, this was like the Japan of the mid-1960s, when also many people responsible for crimes were free and there had been no reconciliation.

She 'feels patriotically Japanese' while also feeling a strong sense of national responsibility for what happened to North Korea, for instance, following the end of Japanese colonial rule in 1945 and the end of the second world war. 'We knew what had been done to us as victims, but what do we know about what we have done to others?', she asked. It is often the case, we agreed, that other countries committed similar war crimes, making Japanese actions not truly exceptional. 'But a crime is a crime', she added, 'we cannot expect to get a pardon just because others committed crimes.' Osa-san said she felt a sense of responsibility for helping to find reconciliation over the second world war: 'It is now seventy years since the war and we are still in turmoil; in thirty years it will be one century. We must find a way by then, and as I am now 50 years old I have to hope I can do something.'

That feeling of responsibility was also important for Sohma Yukika, the founder of AAR and a woman who Osa-san clearly found a great inspiration. Sohma-san was one of the daughters of a prominent liberal politician, Ozaki Yukio, who as mayor of Tokyo was instrumental in a project to send three thousand cherry-tree saplings to Washington, DC, in 1912 as a gift of friendship, to be planted along the Potomac river, which is still graced by the cherry trees and their successors' today. In 2007, Ozaki's then 96-year-old daughter flew to Washington, DC, for America's National Cherry Blossom Festival to commemorate[5] her father's initiative.

Sohma-san spent her career as an English translator—in fact, she was Japan's first simultaneous interpreter between Japanese and English—but also became involved in political reform movements. Osa-san told me it was 'inspiring to hear an older lady talking about politics and about how to reform Japan. She looked very cute and elegant, with her hair in a bonnet, but made a powerful impression when talking about politics.' Sohma-san believed, according to Osa-san, 'that world war two had occurred partly because Japan had been so isolated. She felt it needed to be more part of international society.' So her decision in 1978, at the age of 67, to found AAR (originally called Association to Aid the Indochinese Refugees) was also intended to help Japan to play a bigger role in helping to deal with international crises.

Being part of international society came naturally to Osa-san too. She studied at Waseda University but went to America for her second year at DePeaw University in Indiana. This was during the 1980s. She says she found the college, which is a small liberal arts university, very conservative and had a difficult time there. In fact, she says bluntly, 'I hated America.' Her image of the United States had been that of the big cities such as New York, Chicago, and San Francisco, but the Midwest was a very different place, which she found quite shocking, with even the racist Ku Klux Klan existing among universities there. She recalls a particular 'Catholic priest, and how he dealt with everything without any smile'. Moreover, she felt a strong sense of discrimination against her as an Asian. 'I hadn't previously thought about what it was like being in a minority. I hadn't noticed minorities in Japan before.'

That observation is important, given Osa-san's subsequent interests and career. Following her year in America and once she had

---

[5] 'Nurturing a Legacy of Fleeting Blossoms and Enduring Bonds', *Washington Post*, 8 April 2007.

returned to Waseda, she decided she wanted to study minorities all over the world, including Native Americans and also similar groups in other countries, but realized she ought to begin at home in Japan. As a result, she later spent two years studying the Ainu, Japan's indigenous people, and their lack of involvement in the political life of their communities in Hokkaido, completing her Masters thesis on that topic. While she was conducting her research, one criticism that she says especially hurt her was when some Ainu accused her of 'just doing the research for herself' and not for them or the wider community. When she went back to Tokyo, her professor told her she was wrong to be insulted by this: he said that she should have responded by saying 'yes, I am doing this for myself. But I am also doing it for everyone's knowledge.' The fact that there is no necessary contradiction between self-serving learning and making a wider contribution was an important lesson to her, she said.

Highly attuned to discrimination against minorities, Osa-san emphasized that she 'has never felt discriminated against as a woman'. She did remember her grandmother saying to her that 'women don't have to go to university' but it made no difference to the fact that her parents sent her to Waseda. Many years later, she recalls feeling very annoyed when travelling in a mission in Yugoslavia of UNPROFOR, the UN peacekeeping force, to Gorazde, a town like Srebrenica which was besieged during the war. A lot of bad incidents happened to the mission and one of the soldiers said 'Having women in the ship always makes trouble.' But 'I was very strong at the time and knew what I had to do, so I didn't care.'

On graduation from Waseda, she says she thought about applying to work for the United Nations but felt that there was no real place there at that time for work on indigenous communities. She visited the Ministry of Foreign Affairs and was advised that her best option might be to join a non-profit organization, such as AAR. Yet she knew that the salary would be low and she had no savings to support herself. So instead she got a job at Union Bank of Switzerland in order to build up some savings. After a year she quit that job and borrowed enough money to finance herself through graduate school to do that Masters degree, following which she was able to get a well-paid job as a business analyst for the American firm Dun & Bradstreet, so as to pay off the bank loan.

Such was the path through study and well-paid work that led to Osa-san being able to afford to follow her real passion and to join Sohma-san's AAR in 1990 at a salary that was only one-quarter as much as she had been paid at Dun & Bradstreet. The NPO was then still quite small, being only just over ten years old but it now employs about fifty people. AAR helped her do a doctorate—the PhD on Srebrenica—which also has enabled her ever since to combine academic teaching with refugee work for the NPO.

She worked for AAR full-time until 2003 and then moved to the University of Tokyo to complete her studies and begin teaching, before in 2008 returning to AAR as its president after Sohma-san died. Now she works part-time as president of AAR and part-time as a professor of sociology at Rikkyo University, which is a private university in Ikebukuro in Tokyo. There she teaches students about the Nazi Holocaust as well as about other genocides and war crimes, and the process of bringing about justice for the victims. 'For me, working with AAR is helping living people. In academia, I am helping deceased people. Both are very important to me.'

In fact, at AAR she is helping living people avoid becoming the prematurely deceased of future studies. In that endeavour, she has worked also with Miyoshi Mari. In 1997, when Osa-san took part in the international campaign to ban landmines, Miyoshi-san was her counterpart because she was working in the UN section in the Ministry of Foreign Affairs at the time. Then, much later when a Japanese journalist, Goto Kenji, was kidnapped and killed in Syria in 2015, Osa-san was part of a special small government commission to handle the crisis and Miyoshi-san was again her counterpart, this time as director-general for consular affairs.

Both of these women have a strong sense of justice, both clearly have very determined and intrepid characters, and both seem conscious of the need for Japan to play a role in solving international crises and to reflect upon its own history and decision-making when necessary. Naturally, as a non-diplomat, Osa-san is much freer to state her personal views. In her blog, for example, she offered a thoughtful critique of Japan's policy towards refugees by comparing it with that of President Donald Trump:

> The figure of 50,000 refugees which President Trump, a chauvinist who insists on America First, has announced as a reduced target is 400 times more than the record of Japan's acceptance of refugees in 2015, which was 125 people. Of course, we cannot discuss the difference of figures ignoring the difference in the foundation of the country and the history, or the member of the society. However, are we 400 times more for chauvinism, for being closed, and putting one's country first compared to that President Trump? To question attitudes concerning the acceptance of refugees is to question the form of our country, in my view. In what kind country do we want to live our lives? In what kind of country do you want to die?[6]

---

[6] Unofficial translation by Onoki Kyoko for this book.

9
Discovering, Developing, Teaching

Kuroda Reiko, Nagoya University,
Kawai Eriko, and Ogawa Michiko

All societies have gender stereotypes, with prevailing ideas about what kinds of things men do better and what kinds women do better. They vary from society to society, sometimes contain truth but with exaggeration, sometimes are wholly spurious, and occasionally as with physical attributes are fair if a little misleading. In reality, differences within the genders, between men and men or women and women, are generally more significant than those between the genders.

One quite consistent and persistent theme across the world is nevertheless the notion that females are less good at science and mathematics than men or, to put it in a less qualitative way, that they are less interested in pursuing science studies at school and science-based careers afterwards. But is this true and what does it mean? The question is relevant for Japan, where the representation of women in scientific study or jobs related to science is extremely low. But it is also relevant to other countries, notably the United States, the place where the world's most advanced science is conducted.

In 2006 the President of Harvard University, Larry Summers, was forced to resign[1] as the culmination of a long controversy following a speech[2] he had made a year earlier to an economic conference in

---

[1] 'President of Harvard Resigns, Ending Stormy Five-year Tenure', *New York Times*, 22 February 2006: https://www.nytimes.com/2006/02/22/education/22harvard.html.

[2] Remarks at NBER Conference on Diversifying the Science and Engineering Workforce, Lawrence H. Summers, 14 January 2005: https://web.archive.org/web/20080130023006/http://www.president.harvard.edu/speeches/2005/nber.html.

which he suggested that one of the reasons why women are under-represented in the higher echelons of science could be differences in aptitude. He suggested there might be other reasons too, but this one caused a storm of controversy, especially at a university—one of America's and therefore the world's best—which was supposed to be working hard to build gender equality and other forms of diversity. The result of the storm of protest, within Harvard and around the country, was that this very distinguished economist and academic, who had served as Treasury Secretary in the cabinet of President Bill Clinton, had no real choice but to quit.

The argument did not, of course, go away. Professor Summers had made the mistake of perhaps thinking and speaking too openly, and in a somewhat theoretical, rather academic way. The idea that there could be a genetic difference that explains gender achievements in science is of course theoretically possible, but by drawing attention to the possibility of such an insuperable disadvantage without any actual evidence for it he made many women understandably angry. His other two main hypotheses for why women do not emerge at the top ranks of science in America were less controversial because they apply to other fields of inequality too and imply the presence of free choices: first, he proposed what he called 'the high-powered job hypothesis', namely that fewer young women were willing to commit themselves to a single job involving long hours in the office and total dedication, than were young men; and, second, he wondered whether there were effects of social conditioning and discrimination that might bias females away from scientific fields.

By adding those other two possible explanations, gender inequality in science begins to look a lot less exceptional. The 'high-powered job hypothesis' applies to many fields, including politics, finance, the law, and top corporate careers, especially in a country like Japan where the corporate culture has been one of total commitment. And social conditioning and discrimination also exist in many fields. Very few specialists accept the aptitude-based explanation, for even in the way that Professor Summers expressed it the argument was rather technical. He was not saying that women are less clever than men, but instead that the distribution within the female gender of some characteristics might be different to that for men.

Eileen Pollack, a fellow academic who heard Professor Summers's controversial speech at that economic conference, confronts the issue head on in her 2015 book[3] *The Only Woman in the Room*. She argues that social conditioning, discrimination, and the work culture of scientific laboratories and research departments are the reason for the disparity, not aptitude. No one, as she makes clear, can really know whether there is any genetic issue that makes men likelier to win Nobel prizes in science than women, but everyone should be able to understand that men are simply much likelier for other cultural, social, and institutional reasons to get themselves into a position to be considered for the prize. And as in other fields of study and work, what is more important for most people is the presence of aptitude among both men and women at levels that are still high but not necessarily as exalted as that of Nobel prize winners. Here, she says the evidence is clear: there is no difference in scientific aptitude between men and women.

Ms Pollack's story should be salutary for any Japanese reader as it confirms that the prejudices and misogyny faced by women hoping to pursue an interest in science and engineering are the universal experience of women in the supposedly advanced world. Professor Pollack took an undergraduate degree in physics but then gave up being a scientist to become a full-time writer. She does not regret her life as a writer (and teacher about creative writing) but says she is angry about the way she believes her choice was constrained.

The same sort of thing happens every day in Japan to high school girls and female science undergraduates. Nevertheless, for Japan the issue is, or ought to be, a little different. Books could be written about virtually any field of study or work in Japan with a title like Professor Pollack's: *The Only Woman in the Room*. In America, science (and the related field of software development) looks further behind than other activities in terms of gender equality. In Japan, however, the lack of women in leadership positions in science is not so very different from the lack of women in such positions in the newspaper industry, or banking, or politics, or trading

---

[3] Eileen Pollack, *The Only Woman in the Room: Why Science Is Still a Boy's Club* (Beacon Press, 2015).

companies, or government ministries. The central issues are similar: the barriers women face, and the need for confidence, encouragement, and role models if talented and ambitious women are to overcome them.

Where the prejudice and discrimination about women in science does have a wider impact, nevertheless, is in what it means for access to the top national universities, which in turn has a big impact on women's chances of beginning a career path in a top company or ministry. The National Center Test for University Admissions, which is required for the top national universities in addition to the university's own exam, includes exams in science and mathematics regardless of what major course a student is applying for. For admission to the top private universities, students can generally take exams that match their desired courses. As a result, as Chapter 2 showed, the proportion of females in the top private universities is much higher than at the top national universities.

Under the international assessment of high school students, known as PISA, which is conducted regularly by the Organisation for Economic Co-operation and Development in Paris, the gap between Japanese male and female performance in maths and science is one of the widest among all the advanced countries. In the 2015 PISA tests,[4] female Japanese 15-year-old high school students performed 14 per cent worse than males in both maths and science, while they performed 13 per cent better than boys in English. A discrepancy between male and female performance in science and maths exists in most OECD member countries (though not South Korea, where girls do better than boys in science and maths), but the gap is much wider in Japan. For example, in Britain girls performed 12 per cent worse than boys in the PISA maths test, but only 1 per cent worse in science. In France, girls were 6 per cent worse in maths and just 2 per cent worse in science. In the United States, the gap was 9 per cent in maths and 7 per cent in science.

Cultural preferences and choices made in the family and at high school about studying maths and science are clearly a big explanation for why there are relatively few female Japanese scientists. In the past, another explanation would have been the usual rather

[4] https://www.oecd.org/pisa/pisa-2015-results-in-focus.pdf.

circular one: because there are so few role models of female scientists, this discourages young females from pursuing science, which means that there are too few role models in the next generation too. As in other spheres of life, however, this has gradually been changing. A few women who made their way into science and engineering during the 1970s and 1980s, and who have survived all the usual obstacles, have emerged in leadership positions. Behind them, in the generations that graduated from university in the 1990s and 2000s, there is now a larger group of role models in all sorts of scientific fields, especially medicine and the bio-sciences.

I decided to talk to two women from that earlier generation in science, since both have achieved great prominence in their different fields as scientists. One is a chemist-turned-biologist who spends a lot of her time with snails, studying the genes behind what is called 'chirality' but which essentially means left-handness and right-handedness. The other spends a lot of her time with sounds, for she is both an electrical engineer fascinated by biorhythms and the science of sound, and a professional-standard jazz pianist—as well as being the first and only female board director at Panasonic Corporation in Osaka. Both show a great and infectious enthusiasm for their science and seem to have no regrets at all about having pursued it throughout their careers. They are Kuroda Reiko and Ogawa Michiko. Since education is at the heart of the difficulty young women have faced in making progress not only in science but also other fields, I also visited Nagoya University, which has a reputation of being relatively advanced in its efforts to achieve greater equality under the medical doctor, Matsuo Seiichi, who is its current president, to ask about what can be done to improve matters. And I spoke with another woman who had studied science, in her case environmental studies, who went off and enjoyed an international career in finance, but who then returned to Japan to Kyoto University where she has a role preparing the next generation. Her name is Kawai Eriko.

*   *   *

I met Kuroda Reiko[5] at the Tokyo University of Science, which is where she then had her 'Kuroda Chiromorphology Lab' following

---

[5] Interview with Kuroda Reiko, Tokyo University of Science, 13 July 2017.

her retirement from the University of Tokyo in 2012[6]. She started almost immediately to explain what chiromorphology is and why it matters, and naturally as a non-scientist I found the explanation quite hard to follow. But I concentrated hard and recorded our conversation so that I could listen to her description again later. And when I listened again the explanation was really quite clear. The reason for the difference in my perceptions is that we non-scientists tend to get slightly scared by scientific explanations and so we don't listen very well. We tell ourselves that we won't understand, so we don't really try to do so, tuning out instead. This is probably a mini-version of why high school girls shy away from science. They think they won't understand and won't find it interesting, so they tune out and don't really pay attention.

To be a good listener to science and receptive to it, you might imagine that having parents who are scientists or scientifically literate would help. Perhaps it often does, but in Kuroda-san's case this played no part. Her father was an academic, not in science but in literature. He therefore talked a lot about Noh plays and about philosophy, while his daughter decided she wanted to do something very different: natural science. 'In those days, most people thought women don't do natural sciences', she said. But she was fascinated by chemistry and the way in which the more-than one hundred elements of the Periodic Table react with one another. She later added biology to her expertise, but in pursuit of understanding what determines a particular way in which chemical molecules interact: chirality.

An object is chiral if its mirror image cannot be superimposed upon it. What does this mean? The left foot and the right foot are mirror images of one another, but each fit into their corresponding shoes or socks in an opposite way. That is an observation, but in biology the phenomenon can be important: the chiral way in which molecules are arranged determines whether a plant tendril encircles the branch of a tree, say, in a clockwise or anti-clockwise direction. The point is, it always does it in the same way. Similarly, the shell of a species of snail grows and creates its curl shape in a uniform way. The way in which this happens in different creatures or

---

[6] She has since moved to Chubu University, near Nagoya.

plants is determined by a gene. One of Kuroda-san's most notable achievements has been to identify those genes and to study the way in which chirality is determined in these living organisms. Once you know how it is determined, it becomes possible to intervene in order to change it.

Sometimes this type of biological research requires ingenuity well beyond the scientific field. Kuroda-san told me, with a laugh, that when she and her lab were studying the chirality of giant snails, one of the most difficult tasks was coming up with a tank in which to contain them. Even more difficult, however, in her early career was the attitude of men.

Having studied chemistry at Ochanomizu Women's University, she managed to go to the University of Tokyo to do her PhD. But when it came to thinking about jobs after gaining her doctorate, her supervisor told her that she should get married instead. He even tried to arrange a marriage. Kuroda-san told me 'that I could see that the one academic position that was available would go to a man who had married a relative of my supervisor.' So she feared nepotism as well as misogyny.

As a result, despite not being able to speak much English, she applied for a research post at King's College, London, because there was a professor there whose work she especially admired. 'Fortunately, his post-doctoral researcher quit with thirteen months still left on the grant; I applied for that post and got it.' One characteristic of Britain, even in the 1970s when Kuroda-san was applying for this post, is that although there were plenty of prejudices against women in science and other sources of discrimination, the country acted quite meritocratically when it came to applications by foreigners.

Kuroda-san then lived and worked in Britain for the next ten years in a series of jobs in King's College, London, and other institutes. This built her reputation and skills. Her next move was to apply in 1986 for a job as associate professor at the University of Tokyo: 'I applied not expecting to get the job. But they offered it to me. At last I could be my own boss!' Not just that: six years later she became the first woman to become a full professor in the Natural Sciences department there. 'I was surprised to be first,' she said rather modestly.

Given her great international experience, I asked Kuroda-san how she evaluates the strengths and weaknesses of science at Japanese universities. Rightly, she said that some are doing very well. But her main criticism concerned a lack of the clear use of merit for evaluation and promotion. 'In Japan, people don't want to evaluate other people,' she said, which fits with the widespread use of seniority-based promotion and job rotation rather than merit in many organizations. Moreover, if tuition fees are abolished (as the Abe government has promised), 'it will lead to even less evaluation on grounds of talent.'

Also, she lamented the unwillingness of Japanese universities and research entities to include foreign experts on their selection committees. She pointed to France's Agence Nationale de la Recherche,[7] a government entity that funds scientific research, saying that all the ANR's evaluators are other Europeans, Americans, or Japanese (including her): 'They are not allowed to have any French people,' she said with admiration. 'Could that approach work in Japan?', I asked. 'NO!!' she said emphatically. 'It is even rare for Japanese universities to use external examiners, let alone foreigners.' Rather than embracing internationalization, she said, 'everyone wants an easy life.'

Kuroda-san extended that judgment to her view of female students today. 'I find a general trend, that *both* boys and girls lack ambition,' she said. 'Compared with my day, they are not stopped by parents from doing anything,' but nevertheless still resist trying new things, including speaking English. 'Stereotypes about females do stand in the way, just as they do all over the world,' she said. 'That is why we need role models.'

*   *   *

Kuroda-san is one of those. But why aren't there more? Nagoya University, one of the country's top national universities, has been working especially hard to try to increase its number of female science students and faculty. Its president, Matsuo Seiichi, is a male medical scientist who has been named a 'University Impact Champion' in gender equality by the United Nations Women 'HeforShe' campaign.

---

[7] https://anr.fr.

Nagoya University shares the same features as other top national universities, with medicine, engineering and other science faculties making up a large part of the university—a characteristic that helps explain why female students make up only 30 per cent of under-graduates and postgraduates, which is at least somewhat higher than at other top national colleges. I asked[8] President Matsuo what policies at Nagoya had proven successful in appealing to talented female students and faculty.

Top of his list was an energetic programme to encourage girls at high schools in Aiichi prefecture (the region in which Nagoya sits, famous also for Toyota and other manufacturing giants) to study STEM (science, technology, engineering, and mathematics) subjects, by bringing groups of teenage girls to the university and having them interact with female researchers. They use competitive evaluation methods to help get both students and researchers motivated: 'The high school students give rankings to the researchers for whose work they think is best, and I give an award to the researchers who get the top ranking.' The university also, he said, highlights female researchers on TV and in the press, and gave as one example a female researcher in aircraft engineering who had been written about in local newspapers and held a conference with high school girls as well as their parents.

The university opened a special office for gender equality in 2003, and in 2017 expanded it into a much more ambitious Centre for Gender Equality with its own library and other facilities. They also established in-house nursery schools and after-school activity centres on the campus so that female faculty can bring their chil-dren there and work late if necessary. The after-school activity centre (for children in elementary school) is available until 9pm. The nursery school facilities are quite extensive, but a problem is that the after-school activity centre is much more limited, with space for only fifty children. Clearly, more money and space are both needed. As we have seen before, a big hurdle is finding the staff to be teachers both for nursery and after-school, a shortage 'which is especially severe in this area'. Salaries are low, Matsuo-san

---

[8] Interview with Matsuo Seiichi, Nagoya University, 15 May 2018.

said, and 'most graduates are going to industry and not this kind of occupation.'

In the faculty, females are badly under-represented, which reflects those hurdles about childcare but also the fact that relatively few female students have taken science courses in the past. The proportion of scientific researchers at the university that are female is just 17.4 per cent, which is low, but, he said, 'above the average for other large national universities'. Nagoya is trying an innovative method to try to increase that share. It has begun to experiment with some positions as 'Principal Investigators' that are advertised only to women. These are five-year posts, at the end of which a successful researcher can apply for a full tenured position. 'When we advertise these women-only jobs, we get 30–50 applicants for each position,' he said. "When we advertise normal positions we get very few female applicants.'

Matsuo-san says this approach has been very effective in some areas, notably biology. The head of Nagoya U's biology department is female, and 'she is powerful and is using women-only principal-investigator positions to promote talented females. Now half the faculty in that department are female and are very excellent, as there has been strong competition for posts.' Nevertheless, he admits the effect of this discrimination by using women-only posts has been limited as only a small number of such posts has been available. But he wants to expand their use gradually, until the proportion of females in these positions rises to 30–40 per cent. 'When I became president, I set a goal for 2021, the end of my term, of 20 per cent. By 2027 I want that level raised to 30 per cent. But that would still be a lot lower than in America and Europe.'

Everyone's image of Nagoya is dominated by Toyota and the auto industry. I asked Matsuo-san about employers' attitudes in Aiichi to female workers. He said that yes, as the prefecture is so strong in manufacturing male workers are dominant. But, he added, 'many companies are worrying about their futures, with artificial intelligence, "big data", and other technological trends. Many expect the industrial structure of this area to change during the next five to ten years. There needs to be a change in the way companies do manufacturing, and there is also a severe shortage of workers.' This means, he says, that both industry and local governments are very eager to hire more female workers. The best measures for the future, he says, are to 'change corporate working cultures, and to use advanced technologies to raise efficiency.'

Even traditional and highly successful companies such as Toyota and Denso, he says, 'are always asking us whether we have any female students who might want to work in their company.' Nagoya University's Centre for Gender Equality is, he says, 'collaborating with industry associations to study how best to cultivate those female resources,' helped by a grant from the Ministry of Education (MEXT). Matsuo-san says, in an optimistic final part of our conversation, that he feels sure that working time at Aiichi employers is shortening 'to accommodate changing cultural expectations. I used to work fifteen to sixteen hours a day in the university hospital. Now people are rightly more concerned about their private lives.' That is the sort of attitude that would have been useful at Tokyo Medical University. Systems need to change to adjust to cultural or societal change, rather than fighting against such changes by biasing the results.

*   *   *

Professor Kawai Eriko[9] has not pursued a scientific career, but instead one in finance. However, she is now one of just two female professors (out of twenty) at Kyoto University's new Shishu Kan Graduate School,[10] which offers a rather special five-year PhD programme to just nine or ten students every year in topics related to environmental science, which was Kawai-san's original major. The school's full name is the Graduate School of Advanced Integrated Studies in Human Survivability, and among its missions it declares its intention to educate future leaders. Launched in 2013, if one looks through the list of students enrolled every year one can see quite a clearly male flavour in the early years but now the pictures have become more balanced: in the 2017 enrolment, for example, six out of the nine students were female.

Kawai-san had very conventional educational origins herself at what she describes as an ordinary high school but then she took an

[9] Interview with Kawai Eriko, Imperial Hotel, Tokyo, 3 March 2017.
[10] http://www.gsais.kyoto-u.ac.jp/en-top/wp-content/uploads/2019/05/2020_summer_yoko_sais_e_2.pdf.

unusual step when she saw an advertisement for scholarships for undergraduate studies for Japanese students at Harvard University, offered by the Grew Bancroft Foundation. She had been a top student at her high school and says she could have gone on to the University of Tokyo, but instead she won the Grew Bancroft scholarship and went to America's top private university instead, despite at the time having quite limited knowledge of English. She says she found the first year of her course in environmental studies pretty difficult, but in the end managed to get a good degree. In 1981, after her four years at Harvard, she returned to Japan expecting to get a good job.

What she found was a rigid system that wasn't welcoming either to Japanese who had studied abroad or to women. Having graduated in America and having spent the next two months travelling in France, she had missed the annual job recruitment period for Japanese corporations by the time she got to Japan. She eventually managed to get a post at Nomura Research Institute. The achievement was, however, bitter-sweet, as many women of her generation will recognize: at NRI despite her Harvard degree and fluent English she was given a uniform to wear and made to serve tea. Moreover, she was told right at the outset that she would have to leave the company when she got married, so it was clear NRI would not invest any effort in developing her career.

After three years at NRI Kawai-san decided to quit and to attempt a repeat of her successful international educational experience. She chose to take an MBA course so as to launch a career in business and picked the Insead Business School in France. She says she felt it would be easier as a Japanese to fit in in Europe as it is less cut-throat and aggressive than the United States. She financed herself through a one-year MBA at Insead, graduated in 1985, and fortunately found that by then people with knowledge of Japan and Japanese were in high demand among foreign firms. She started off with a job at the McKinsey consulting firm in Paris but switched to finance by becoming a fund manager at the S. G. Warburg investment bank in London.

This international career did not get in the way of marriage, despite what Nomura had said. Kawai-san's husband worked for the

Tokyo Marine & Fire insurance company, and he followed her to Europe. The couple succeeded in having thoroughly international—or perhaps I should say, European—careers in France, the UK, Poland, and Switzerland, where both husband and wife got jobs at the Bank for International Settlements, a special international institution which serves central banks. But having had such a successful career, Kawai-san says she started to think about retirement from finance and finding something different to do.

That is how she ended up as a professor at Kyoto University, sharing her international perspective with students while returning to her original field of environmental studies. I asked for her impressions of Japan on returning after nearly thirty years working abroad. She said, with some sadness, that she has felt rather as if she was returning in time, back to the beginning of the 1980s, because so many procedures and practices seemed not to have changed since that time.

If we want to understand why in the post-bubble period Japan has experienced such slow growth in productivity, a good place to start is the sort of system Kawai-san cites at her university for getting approval just for one trip to Tokyo: the authorization needs ten *hanko* stamps, which probably means it is passing through ten people. Similar procedures can be found in all sorts of service sectors, including banks and insurance, lawyers and media companies as well as educational institutions. While manufacturing companies have been able constantly to improve their processes, under the pressure of competition, too many service companies and public institutions have remained conservative, rigid and, truly, stuck in the pre-digital era. We can but hope that the future leaders that the Shishu-Kan produces will be able to modernize the various institutions in which they spend their careers. And the 2020 pandemic provided another hope: that the pressures of extreme necessity might force institutions to modernise their procedures and jump from the *hanko* era to the digital one.

∗   ∗   ∗

Ogawa Michiko[11] is remarkable in all sorts of ways, but one of the most remarkable parts of her career story is that she is a Japanese

---

[11] Interview with Ogawa Michiko, Panasonic Corporation, Osaka, 1 March 2017.

woman who decided to stay working for her company because of her private life. She stayed because she wanted to get married, rather than following the stereotype by leaving for exactly that reason.

How could that be? The reason is that at a crucial point in her career at Panasonic, at the age of 42, she found herself facing a choice between her private life in Japan and a great professional offer abroad. The great professional offer was a proposal that she should quit the company and go to America as a professional jazz musician. Since her passion is the piano, she must have been tempted. But a couple of years beforehand she had been reunited with the man who had been her first boyfriend in her schooldays, and with whom she had lost touch. They decided to get married. That is why she turned down the chance to become a touring professional jazz pianist and chose to stay at Panasonic in Osaka instead. And that is why she is now Panasonic's only female executive board director and is head of the Technics audio brand.

Her first board meeting in August 2015, she told me, 'was very strange for me. But I didn't feel any stress or isolation.' Nevertheless, with a laugh, she said that a board meeting is still 'more stressful than a jazz performance' as it is all quite theoretical rather than emotional. At the end of that first meeting, in the bar after dinner, the chairman asked her to play some jazz at the piano. She complied, taking requests from other board members and felt a lot more relaxed as a result. She says she now always plays the piano after board events. One thing's for sure: playing jazz to your male colleagues is quite different from serving them tea. Yes, she is entertaining them. But this may well make them feel subservient to her, and more than a little envious of her talent, rather than the other way around.

She certainly thinks the world in which Panasonic is operating is changing, and that firms like hers need to change with it. In the past, the firm was 'very hardware-focused. Now we see the need for a more holistic, all-round approach. Recently, artificial intelligence and robotics are becoming the standard format in the consumer appliances sector, and we need to push this game-changer for the future. So, it is the right timing for me to join the board.' It is a world in which the sort of multi-tasking that women are said to be particularly good at has become more vital, she says, as software and hardware have become more and more integrated.

Appropriately, my meeting with Ogawa-san began with us listening to music. She and her colleagues took me to a special sound studio where they demonstrated top-of-the-range Technics equipment, the most expensive of which cost $50,000. It was all impressive, made more so when I was told that that sort of Technics equipment is now used in the famous Abbey Road Studios in London where many Beatles albums were recorded in the 1960s, and that the team is doing a special collaboration with the Berlin Philharmonic Orchestra. It is all very high end and sophisticated.

When we moved to a more conventional meeting room, she told me she felt she had essentially had three different careers at Panasonic, before her current one in charge of reviving the Technics brand. She began in 1986 as a recording engineer, before moving later to the network service business and then working on Corporate Social Responsibility. That is a function which by the late 1990s had become expected of major multinational companies and which, as she told me, fitted perfectly with the philosophy handed down by Matsushita Konosuke, the firm's founder.

Technics has an odd story by the standards of corporate brands. It had its heyday in the 1960s and 1970s during the analogue era of vinyl records and turntables; then in the 1980s and 1990s when Ogawa-san worked for it the mission was to improve the digital sound that had come in with CDs (compact discs) so that it was as good as analogue. But then the Internet revolutionized audio listening yet again, degrading sound quality as it did so but also making music a much more casual affair, particularly once smartphones took hold. As a result, the Technics brand was suspended in 2004. Panasonic stopped manufacturing high-end audio equipment, although it carried on making just one product, a turntable for DJs, until 2010.

It is rare for corporate brands to be revived once they have been suspended for so long. But Panasonic felt that an opportunity was opening up again to sell to audiophiles at the very high end of the market, as most listening had become rather commoditized and routine. In 2014 the firm decided to relaunch Technics, and Ogawa-san re-entered that team in May of that year. She says, with some excitement, that her team had only four months before the planned announcement of the relaunch in September. 'I could not sleep and had no private time at all, no Sundays for four months, as we worked to improve, improve, improve. Those four months were the most intense and concentrated period of my career.'

In fact, she said that 'all my career was focused on those four months.' I can see what she meant: her ability to lead and manage a team of specialists under great pressure; her ability to concentrate professionally on the immediate task; and most of all her interest in the science of sound. That interest had manifested itself first of all at Keio University where she majored in electronics and chose to study in the acoustic research laboratory. She says she was 'interested in the effect of sound and music on biology and on medicine'. In her electronics class she recalls that there were five or six other women, who took jobs at firms like Sony and NTT, just as she did with Panasonic. 'They gave up when they had children. I carried on because I knew I love this science, this work.'

I finished by asking Ogawa-san what her ambitions were for the next ten years. She began by saying she very much wanted to make Technics a great success. The team has two target markets: one is audiophiles; the other is music lovers. She says that audiophiles are basically centred on the equipment while music lovers are naturally music-centric. Technics's task is to narrow the gap between the two segments, especially by educating the music lover about the importance of their devices and of taking care of them. The hope is to develop what she called the 'casual high end', which I take to mean a consumer who wants to listen to audio in a casual manner, but on very high-quality devices and is wealthy enough to do so.

Her other ambition is a wider and larger one, outside her company. She 'would like to change the male power hierarchy in Japan'. Not all on her own, of course, but she thinks 'many female executives think the same and have sympathy with this goal. They sometimes feel a little isolated, a little distanced, a little gap between their real situation and their ideal goal'. And Ogawa-san does think that 'company culture will change gradually in Japan'.

The question one is left with is this: is gradual change good and fast enough?

PART THREE

CONCLUSIONS AND RECOMMENDATIONS

10
The Tasks Ahead

On the face of it, Japan is in pretty good shape. Its crime rates are among the lowest in the world even allowing for the likelihood that sexual violence is considerably under-reported and under-investigated in this still misogynistic country. But if you leave a wallet or purse, bulging with cash, in a restaurant, taxi, train, or bus even in a big city the chance is high that you will get it back, with nothing missing. This is also one of the most stable societies in the world, one in which disturbances are virtually unknown and even strikes or demonstrations are rare. The nation's life expectancy is the world's highest for any sizeable country; if it weren't for natural disasters, in the form of the earthquakes, tsunami, typhoons, floods, and landslides that have been a feature of Japanese life and death since time immemorial, the country would feel almost preternaturally safe.

One reason why the 2011 Fukushima nuclear meltdown that followed the tragic earthquake and tsunami was so unnerving was that it seemed abruptly to overturn the prevailing sense of a well-governed, well-regulated society in which anything that could have been done to limit the potential risks from earthquakes would have been done. That nuclear disaster led to residents and visitors alike distrusting foodstuffs from some areas and carrying potassium iodide pills in case of radiation leakage. The clean-up of that Fukushima nuclear plant will take decades. Yet after a brief dip following the disaster the number of foreigners visiting Japan each year[1] has soared from 8.6 million visits in 2010 to more than

---

[1] JTB Tourism Research and Consulting: https://www.tourism.jp/en/tourism-database/stats/inbound/#annual.

31 million in 2018. And there is plenty of scope for further growth: this still placed Japan far behind such countries as France (86 million in 2017), China (60 million), Italy (58 million), or even the United Kingdom (37 million) in terms of annual tourist arrivals. The shock and the fear associated with the 2020 covid-19 pandemic halted tourism in its tracks in Japan just as in other countries, but once a vaccine has been successfully produced and distributed visitor numbers can again be expected to revive and to renew their growth.

Living standards[2] in Japan remain good if not at the chart-beating levels they were at when *Heisei* began: in 2017 Japan's GDP per capita ranked 28th in the world at then current exchange rates, or 33rd if adjusted for differences in domestic purchasing power, placing Japan just below both France and the United Kingdom. On the United Nations Human Development Index, which encompasses a wider range of measures beyond economics including education and life expectancy, Japan ranked 19th, placing it below the United States and the United Kingdom but ahead of France. As already noted in Chapter 2 of this book, it is on gender inequality that Japan ranks really poorly, being 121st out of 153 countries in the World Economic Forum's latest assessment.[3] Yet notwithstanding such inequality, and despite the economic shocks and declines in income and job security seen in the 1990s and 2000s, remarkably few Japanese citizens, male or female, have emigrated in search of jobs or better lives elsewhere, unlike in the late nineteenth and early twentieth centuries when many left for the United States and Brazil. According to the Statistics Bureau of Japan,[4] in 2016 there were just 1.34 million Japanese nationals living abroad, which is roughly the same as merely the number of British nationals living in the twenty-seven European Union countries, for a country nearly twice the UK's population. The total had increased by just 20,000 compared with 2015. A Pew Research poll[5] in 2018 showed that considerably

---

[2] All living standards data from *The Economist Pocket World in Figures*, 2020 edition (Profile Books, 2019).

[3] World Economic Forum Global Gender Gap Report 2020, published 2019: https://www.weforum.org/reports/gender-gap-2020-report-100-years-pay-equality.

[4] https://www.stat.go.jp/english/data/nenkan/67nenkan/1431–02.html.

[5] https://www.pewresearch.org/global/2018/11/12/perceptions-of-immigrants-immigration-and-emigration/.

more Japanese were worried about emigration than about immigration, making Japan probably the only advanced country about which that can currently be said.

Classically, or to some notoriously, the Japanese often distinguish between surface appearances, or *tatemae*, and the truth, *honne*. The *honne* is also good for Japan by comparison with other countries, but it contains some important and worrying vulnerabilities that are often concealed by the neat-and-shiny *tatemae*. Demography is at the heart of those vulnerabilities. This is a country with no natural resources barring the energy and brainpower of its people, but they are getting steadily older and gradually fewer. With the highest median age[6] of any country in the world bar Monaco, at 47.1 in 2017, with 28.2 per cent of the population over the age of 65, and with the total population now falling by 500,000 per year, Japan's public and private finances alike are inevitably going to remain stretched, dominated by the need to finance pensions and healthcare and hampered by weakness in tax revenues. Depopulation is not intrinsically disastrous, but by eating away at tax revenues and undermining asset values for anyone who owns residential property it is bound to make life harder. Other objectives, whether they be better lifelong education, scientific research, overseas aid or stronger defence, will always find it difficult to compete for public funds.

Japan has since 1990 proved that to carry what is by far the world's largest government debt in proportion to GDP[7] is entirely possible, even for decades at a time, if you can finance it domestically, which is increasingly done through central bank money creation. But the debt is nevertheless a sign of weakness and the current structure of public finances cannot be sustained indefinitely. The debt is not the result of any sort of public extravagance. Japanese public spending is low by global standards: at about 39 per cent[8] of GDP in recent years it has been slightly above American

---

[6] *The Economist Pocket World in Figures*, 2020 edition.
[7] In 2019, gross government debt was 237 per cent of GDP in 2019 by IMF measures while net of government financial assets it was a little over 140 per cent. Both gross and net it is the world's largest as a share of GDP, ahead of Greece and Italy: https://www.imf.org/external/datamapper/GGXWDG_NGDP@WEO/OEMDC/ADVEC/WEOWORLD/JPN.
[8] https://data.oecd.org/gga/general-government-spending.htm.

levels and far below most European levels which range between 40–55 per cent of GDP. Just below one-quarter[9] of public expenditure is devoted to servicing the debt, even at today's extraordinarily low interest rates. And the ratio of tax to GDP[10] is also low: at 31.4 per cent in 2017 it was a little higher than for the United States but well below the OECD average. Tax revenues have stubbornly failed to rise markedly despite repeated attempts to widen the tax base by raising indirect taxes and to stimulate economic growth through monetary expansion. A main reason for that is that the household incomes and consumption on which tax is principally levied have themselves remained stubbornly depressed, regardless of levels of employment. In 2017,[11] tax and stamp revenues produced 59.2 per cent of government income (including bond issuance), of which 46.5 percentage points came from taxes levied on individuals.

Why have household incomes and consumption remained depressed? A nation once famed for its high household savings ratio is now a nation of citizens who cannot afford to save: according to OECD data,[12] Japanese households saved 13.28 per cent of their net disposable incomes in 1994 but only 2.75 per cent of disposable income in 2017. The stock of household financial assets remains large, thanks to past saving habits, but the flow of new savings is now meagre. The explanation lies in a shift in bargaining power between firms and workers that took hold during the worst of the post-bubble period but has become entrenched thanks to the emergence of the dual labour market divided between secure regular workers and insecure non-regular workers on poorly paid short-term and part-time contracts.

The nearly two-fifths of the labour force that is on those non-regular contracts benefits from little training, builds up little relevant experience and so represents a chronic under-use and even depletion of human capital. The largest part—two-thirds—of that

---

[9] Ministry of Finance Public Finance Fact Sheet, 2017: https://www.mof.go.jp/english/budget/budget/fy2017/04.pdf.

[10] https://www.oecd.org/tax/revenue-statistics-japan.pdf.

[11] Ministry of Finance Public Finance Fact Sheet, 2017: https://www.mof.go.jp/english/budget/budget/fy2017/04.pdf.

[12] https://data.oecd.org/hha/household-savings.htm.

under-used and depleted human capital of non-regular workers consists of women. But the one-third that are men include, as we saw in Chapter 1, men in the 'ice age generation' of 1993–2004 when regular jobs were hard to find for new high-school and even university graduates and who now still suffer from their lack of training, from the difficulty of joining larger companies mid-career, and from their lack of pension provision.

These phenomena of job insecurity, of under-used and depleted human capital, and of depressed incomes find their counterparts in one economic trend and one social trend. The economic trend is of productivity growth that has slowed even as technology advances and even as labour has become scarce. Wage growth has been even slower: on the OECD's reckoning,[13]

Real wages have lagged behind labour productivity growth over the past 25 years, reflecting in part the increasing proportion of low-paid non-regular workers. The gap between productivity and wage growth since 1990 in Japan is more than double the OECD average.

But also productivity growth itself has been poor: according to the OECD,[14] labour productivity in Japan is a quarter below that of the top half of OECD countries (among which it used to be ranked) and growth in what the organization calls 'multifactor productivity', i.e. the efficiency with which all sorts of inputs are used, more than halved between 2000–7 and 2007–15. The OECD attributes this poor performance to a widening disparity in productivity between different firms, to declining business dynamism, as measured by low start-up and exit rates, and to an increasing misallocation of resources. The share of GDP taken by labour relative to that taken by capital (i.e. firms' profits) fell by 'about 6 percentage points over 1995–2014, the fifth largest decline in the OECD, with most of it in services. The shrinking labour share is due in part to the rise in non-regular employment.'[15]

[13] *OECD Survey of Japan 2017*, pp. 21–2.
[14] *OECD Survey of Japan 2017*, pp. 79–80.
[15] *OECD Survey of Japan 2017*, pp. 82–3.

With that sort of misuse of human capital, Japan has moved from being a relatively high-wage economy at the end of the 1980s with most employees enjoying high levels of job security and a high sense of economic equality, to a relatively low-wage economy now with a much greater level of inequality, especially in terms of job security. This applies to both men and women. As the OECD observes,[16] Japan's share of households in relative poverty despite having two or more workers is the second highest in the OECD.

This brings us to the counterpart social trend: a declining rate of marriage and, in direct connection with that, a persistently low fertility rate. Japan now has the 25th lowest marriage rate[17] in the world, with four marriages per 1,000 people in 2017, compared with, for example, 6.9 in the United States. In the early 1990s, Japan's marriage rate was about 6.0 per 1,000; by 2011[18] it was 5.5. By 2015, nearly one-quarter of men aged 50 had never been married and nearly 15 per cent of women[19] (see also Figure 1.10). In other countries, declining rates of marriage do not necessarily imply declining fertility because co-habitation and single parenthood may be common, but not in Japan where both are rare: fewer marriages mean fewer children. To get married requires not just a partner but sufficient financial security to be able to reassure that partner—in the case of men—or to be able to afford the costs of raising children, in the case of double-income households. As we saw in Chapter 1, Professor Kato Akihiko of Meiji University has established[20] that there is a direct link between lack of secure resources and decisions not to marry or not to have children.

Japan's vulnerability can also therefore be seen as a kind of gently but remorselessly vicious cycle: while the ageing and shrinking of

---

[16]   *OECD Survey of Japan 2017*, p. 78.

[17]   *The Economist Pocket World in Figures*, 2020 edition.

[18]   *The Economist Pocket World in Figures*, 2014 edition.

[19]   *Statistical Handbook of Japan* (Statistics Bureau, 2019): https://www.stat.go.jp/english/data/handbook/index.html.

[20]   Kato Akihiko, *Two Major Factors behind the Marriage Decline in Japan: The Deterioration in Macroeconomic Performance and the Diffusion of Individualism Ideology*, paper delivered at Population Association of America Annual Meeting 2012: https://paa2012.princeton.edu/abstracts/121688. Also published in *Journal of Population Problems* 67.2 (2011).

its population is becoming more entrenched thanks to low marriage and fertility rates, the country's use of its basic resource, the human capital embodied by a well-educated population, looks stuck in a trap of surprisingly low wages, insecure work, and low productivity, which in turn depresses domestic spending and tax revenues while also suppressing marriage and fertility. The trumpeted reforms of 'Abenomics', implemented since Abe Shinzo's return to the prime ministership in December 2012, have provided monetary and fiscal fuel so as to keep the economic engines running but have so far failed to find transformative solutions for low wages, job insecurity, and low productivity, or for declining marriage rates and low fertility.

Yet alongside this persistent vulnerability and economic and social strain has nevertheless arisen something new and potentially transformative. This is the surge in access to full university education by women during the 1990s and 2000s, growing from only 10–12 per cent of 18-year-old females attending four-year university courses in the mid-1980s to over 50 per cent now and virtually closing the educational gender gap with their male counterparts. In that way, Japan's human capital has become greatly enhanced compared with past decades.

This enhanced human capital is nevertheless being severely under-used. But that under-use is not inevitable. The pipeline of women available to take up leadership roles of all kinds, which was once meagre, is now growing, especially among women currently in their 30s and 40s, which in turn raises the possibility that a critical mass of those female leaders may be able to induce changes in corporate practices that in turn improve the use of that human capital, both female and male.

In a paper[21] in 2013 for the Japan Institute for Labour Policy and Training, Margarita Estevez-Abe of Syracuse University attributed the then prevailing gender gap to the country's quite rigid labour-market institutions, to women's lower social status than in other

---

[21] Margarita Estevez-Abe, *An International Comparison of Gender Equality: Why Is the Japanese Gender Gap So Persistent?*, *Japan Labor Review* (Spring 2013): https://www.jil.go.jp/english/JLR/documents/2013/JLR38_estevez-abe.pdf.

advanced countries, to barriers to outsourcing domestic child and elderly care, to the strong role companies play in occupational training, to discrimination in the workplace, and to the lack of an unambiguous government commitment to take action through spending on childcare or use of affirmative action. The question now, for 2020 and beyond, is how much has changed and how much can be changed, if the government and corporate managements were to show a commitment to do so.

Two measures the Abe government has succeeded in implementing that will help more of these women to be candidates for influential roles are the expansion of publicly funded or subsidized childcare facilities and the Work-Style Reform Bill that came into effect in April 2019, both described in Chapter 2. As Estevez-Abe identified, a lack of childcare facilities has been a big hindrance to women's careers in a country in which the multi-generational households for which it was once renowned, and which provided grandparents on tap to look after children while mothers worked in the fields, are now rare. Long hours of overtime working and corporate socializing have also kept managerial advancement essentially a male domain, while contributing to troubling phenomena such as death by overwork, *karoshi*, even as productivity in service-sector occupations has remained poor. If the Work-Style Reform Bill's limits on overtime can be firmly enforced and can contribute to a broad rethink among managements about how to modernize the way work and staff are organized and motivated, it could have the dual benefit of boosting productivity and enabling more women to qualify themselves for managerial roles. The Reform Bill may also at least begin to alter the unconscious gender biases shown in companies albeit while leaving conscious discrimination still in place. Even so, despite those welcome measures, the government's commitment to gender equality and diversity cannot yet be described as unambiguous.

What we have seen in the seven chapters of Part Two, through the stories of the twenty-one successful women interviewed, is that Japan now certainly has the sort of diversity of experience for women that Gill Steel of Doshisha University and her co-authors wrote about in 'Beyond the Gender Gap in Japan'.[22] This emergence of role models of many kinds, in all sorts of fields and often with quite a high degree of public prominence, is helping to reduce the problem of social status identified by Estevez-Abe, or at least its correlate, a lack of confidence among women. Diversity has become a fashionable mantra about which it is easy to be sceptical but official requirements that companies disclose a wide range of data have helped to make the mantra appear serious. As and when more women arrive in decision-making roles in companies and other organizations, that talk of diversity will turn far more into action, with human resources policies beginning to be modernized.

*   *   *

The benefit of reducing insecurity among men and women, and greatly increasing gender equality and diversity, would be big. Japan could become a country in which the last but greatest social injustice had been eliminated or—to be fair—reduced to the same sort of level as is found in Western Europe and North America. It could become a country in which the human capital built up in an excellent education system was being put to as productive a use as its owners—the women and men of Japan—want it to be. A country in which that use of human capital is rewarded with high wage levels, high living standards, and high quality goods and services, making it akin to being the Switzerland of Asia. A country in which secure jobs and good public and corporate childcare facilities cause a revival both in marriage and in the birth rate, slowing the decline in population. A country in which thanks to higher incomes and stronger household consumption, tax revenues rise sufficiently to permit a steady reduction in the public debt.

What needs to be done to achieve this is not dramatic or even revolutionary in nature, but it will require much greater government commitment to gender equality and to labour-market reforms, and a widespread commitment in the private sector to modernizing recruitment and staff-development practices to suit

---

[22] *Beyond the Gender Gap in Japan*, Michigan Monograph Series in Japanese Studies 85, ed. Gill Steel (2019).

an era of declining population and changing mores. Here is a potential and feasible agenda for public policy and private actions to be able to secure this benefit.

Public policy measures

1. Raise the minimum wage sharply

Many interventions take time to implement or to have an effect. But one tool that government can use to have an immediate effect on wage rates and so on household incomes and expenditure is the national minimum wage. Currently, Japan's minimum wage is among the lowest in the advanced countries. There is a national level set by an advisory committee of the Ministry of Labour on the basis of which prefectures set their own levels. In 2019 those levels varied between Y761 per hour in Kagoshima on Kyushu island and Y985 in Tokyo,[23] giving an average minimum nationwide of Y874, which the ministry's advisory panel then increased by 3.1 per cent on 31 July 2019 to Y901. At an exchange rate of Y108 to the US dollar that is just $8.34 per hour or at Y143 to the pound sterling it is just £6.30. The UK minimum wage for adults in 2019 was £8.21 per hour, equivalent to Y1,165 per hour. The US federal minimum wage is $7.25 per hour, but only twenty-four of the fifty states abide by the federal rate.[24] Fifteen states set minimum wages at $10 per hour or higher.

There are legitimate concerns that a sharp rise in the minimum wage could in some circumstances lead to a rise in unemployment. However, at a time when labour is scarce this objection falls away. With relative poverty levels high and a large number of non-regular workers earning the minimum wage, a bold government would seek to raise the national average minimum quite sharply, even to Y1,500 per hour. A 50 per cent rise in one year would cause too much of a shock to employers, but a rise to Y1,500 per hour phased

[23] https://resources.realestate.co.jp/living/what-is-the-minimum-wage-in-japan-2019-ranking-by-prefecture/.
[24] https://www.paycor.com/resource-center/minimum-wage-by-state.

in over three years, to be followed by further rises thereafter, would give companies and public sector employers time to react. At a stroke, this would boost consumer spending and would make non-regular work feel more viable and even dependable. It would also reduce the gender pay gap, since many women work at the minimum wage.

2. Reform labour laws to reduce or eliminate the divide between regular and non-regular contracts

The single most important task for public policy is further labour law reform, even beyond the Work-Style Reform Bill that the Abe administration was proud of achieving in 2018. Contrary to Prime Minister Abe's stated ambition, that 2018 bill will not eliminate the term 'non-regular' because although equal pay for equal work could remedy one of the disadvantages of part-time and temporary contracts it will not confront the most important issues: the insecurity of those contracts and the lack of incentive they give both to employers and employees to invest money and effort in training or skills development. In reality, non-regular is a synonym for 'insecure'.

To ban or restrict non-regular work would be to deny companies and employees much needed flexibility. What is needed instead is the development of a sort of halfway house between fully protected regular contracts and highly precarious non-regular ones, by developing and popularizing a form of contractual security that gives both employers and employees enough assurance that each is committed to the other, without the relationship needing to become totally permanent and expensive. The best solution is one that has been proposed by the American Chamber of Commerce in Japan:[25] a new type of labour contract that is, in effect, a halfway house between regular and non-regular employment, offering employment that has no pre-determined duration but for which a pre-agreed severance-payment formula would apply, depending on how

---

[25] *Untapped Potential*: White Paper by ACCJ Women in Business committee 2016: https://www.accj.or.jp/uploads/4/9/3/4/49349571/2016_wib_whitepaper_e.pdf.

many years of service the employee had put in before termination. A similar proposal was made in an IMF Working Paper in 2013, 'The Path to Higher Growth: Does Revamping Japan's Dual Labor Market Matter?'.[26]

Previous efforts to enact such contractual rights have foundered on difficulties of interpretation by the courts of severance payment rights which has hindered the spread of such contracts. So the law would have to be especially carefully drafted. Such a contract should make it easier to join companies in mid-career, or to return to work after an extended child-raising break. The known severance payment would help reduce or remove the risk of not being able to find another job, especially if it can be expected to be received immediately rather than after a lengthy review by the courts. A further necessary reform is to make employees' pension rights transferrable between companies, since otherwise job mobility comes at too high a risk for employees. It is the relative rigidity of the labour market that has allowed or encouraged non-regular employment to flourish, for it provided the only available form of flexibility.

3.   Eliminate the marriage tax completely

A minor reform that was implemented in 2017 was an adjustment to the income threshold below which working spouses can remain considered as dependent on their husbands and therefore gain associated tax benefits. As was explained in Chapter 2, the threshold was raised from Y1.03m a year to Y1.5m. This large jump from a very low level was portrayed as an important new incentive for more married woman to go out to work and earn more, but in fact it is not.

The threshold of Y1.5m remains very low, being equivalent to earnings of just Y125,000 per month or Y6,250 per working day. That is simply a seven-hour working day at the national minimum wage. If it has any effect at all, this threshold incentivizes married women to work part-time on low incomes because if they get a

---

[26]   Aoyagi Chie and Giovanni Ganelli, IMF Working Paper WP/13/202.

properly paid job they and their families will be penalised by the tax system. This is in effect a marriage tax, or more strictly a tax on work within marriage. Raising the threshold has not changed that basic fact.

A far better reform would be to abolish this income threshold completely and instead to allow married couples to choose whether to be taxed separately or jointly, providing the same tax allowances to both. When both husband and wife work, it will most often be beneficial to them to be taxed separately, so as to avoid being taxed at higher marginal income tax rates. This also means, however, that both of them, which mainly means the wife, would then have every reason to get a well-paid job commensurate to her qualifications and skills with no points on the income scale at which her tax or social security burden would suddenly jump. This would generally mean that she would earn a much higher income, and so would pay the government more income tax. The family as a whole would then be better off, and so would be the government.

4.   Redouble public spending on childcare facilities to achieve universal provision

As previously noted, a welcome achievement of the Abe administration since 2012 has been the improved provision of publicly funded or subsidized childcare facilities. The total capacity of day-care centres has increased from 2.2 million places in 2012 to more than 2.8 million in 2018.[27] However, demand for places has also increased, as more families find that using daycare facilities is socially acceptable. This strongly suggests that despite all the constraints on public spending, a further big increase in spending on childcare facilities is going to be necessary.

Germany, a country with a similar demographic profile to Japan's as well as sharing many of the traditional social stigmas against single parenthood and combining work with child-raising, has succeeded in raising its fertility rate quite impressively in recent years.

---

[27] Goldman Sachs, Womenomics 5.0 Report, April 2019.

The main mechanisms appear to have been a big increase in daycare provision and a determined effort to persuade husbands to take up their paternity leave entitlements in order to set in train a rebalancing of gender roles inside the family. In 2013 the German government declared a universal right to nursery places for all children over 1 year old and since then has been trying to make reality fit that declaration. It is too soon to be sure that fertility rates will continue to rise or that gender roles will continue to evolve towards a more even balance, but the early signs are modestly encouraging.[28] Germany's fertility rate has risen from 1.33 per adult woman in the mid-2000s to 1.57 in 2019, bringing it close to the European Union average. Some of the rise can be attributed to the immigration of people from countries with higher birth rates, but much has also been driven by a rise in daycare availability.[29]

Japan's fertility rate has recovered a little to 1.42 in recent years (see Figure 1.11), but that is too little to arrest or even slow the shrinkage of total population. But if marriage and early family formation can be made more viable again, by a combination of improving the security of employment, achieving a much more widespread availability of childcare, and using paternity leave to inspire a change in the balance of household roles, the demographic destiny of Japan can be changed. The impact of even quite small changes in the fertility rate on the country's future population are shown in projections made by the National Institute of Population and Social Security Research. The institute's latest report, published in 2017,[30] used three alternative assumptions about fertility: low fertility, defined as the rate of births per woman falling back to 1.2, its 2005 low point; medium fertility, defined as the rate remaining at the 2015 level of 1.45; and high fertility defined as the rate rising to 1.66 by 2024 and staying there. For 2065, the low fertility rate produced a population of 82 million; the medium option a population of 88 million; and the high option 95 million.

[28] DeutscheWelle:https://www.dw.com/en/are-family-policy-reforms-to-thank-for-germanys-rising-birth-rates/a-43188961.
[29] *The Economist*, 29 June 2019: https://www.economist.com/europe/2019/06/29/why-germanys-birth-rate-is-rising-and-italys-isnt/
[30] Population Projections for Japan 2016–65: http://www.ipss.go.jp/pp-zenkoku/e/zenkoku_e2017/pp_zenkoku2017e.asp.

There is thus already a difference of 13 million people in four decades' time between these low and high birth rate assumptions. And the 'high' fertility assumption is not really all that high. A recovery to 1.66 would raise Japan's fertility rate only to about the same level as it currently is in the European Union as a whole and back merely to the level it was at in Japan in about 1990. In Sweden the rate is 1.88, in Ireland 1.97 and in France 2.07. There is no reason in principle why Swedish, Irish, or French levels could not be achievable in a country that is culturally as family-friendly as Japan.

5. Reduce the gender bias in national university admissions

The top national universities are the main pathways to leadership careers in government and the private sector. But less than one-third of students at those universities are female compared with 44 per cent at the top private universities and 50 per cent at most equivalent prestigious universities in Europe or America. All the national universities have targets for increasing their share of female students, but progress towards them is slow. Progress could be accelerated if the National Center Test that is required and set by the Ministry of Education[31] for admission to public universities could be altered to remove the requirement that all students take exams in maths and science even if they are applying for non-science courses.

That would place the national test in line with the exams used by most (but not all) private universities, which allow candidates to select exam subjects according to their choice of degree, and would remove an admissions bias which itself reflects a bias against science and mathematics among girls in high school. It will take far longer to remove the bias among girls at school, allowing an accelerated move towards equality at university.

---

[31] The ministry's full title is the Ministry of Education, Culture, Sports, Science, and Technology, abbreviated to MEXT: https://www.mext.go.jp/en/.

6.   Reform visa and work permit rules to allow recruitment of foreign domestic help

According to Osawa Machiko,[32] director of the Research Institute for Women and Careers located at Japan Women's University in Tokyo, a crucial issue for decisions by married couples over whether or not to have children are the working hours of the husband. 'For as long as the husband plays a zero role at home, getting home at around 10 or 11 o'clock at night, and then leaving early the next morning, it is going to be very hard for women to combine work and family,' she says. For the vast majority of families, the important change is therefore both a cultural one, about men's roles, and a corporate one, about overtime and drinking with colleagues.

There is, however, another issue, which if it were solved would help a great deal, especially for families that are able to earn fairly good incomes. This is the ability to hire nannies, au pairs, or maids to help with childcare and other domestic chores and responsibilities. This is already possible, of course, as the discussion of Nakamura-san's business, Poppins, showed in Chapter 5. But it is expensive and difficult, because of the same labour shortage that makes it both desirable and possible for more women to go out to work. The simplest solution would be for the government to liberalize the immigration rules for foreign nannies, au pairs, and maids.

The absurdity of the current law is that expatriate families are permitted to import foreign maids, but not Japanese families. If this were changed, it could have a dramatic effect on the ability of young Japanese couples to have children. This does not need to involve long-term immigration: the great thing about au pairs and nannies is that they are often highly motivated to come to learn the language just for a few years, rather than to earn lots of money or to become permanent residents. Such a desire should be able to be accommodated by a new law amending the immigration rules enacted in late 2018 by the Diet so as to add domestic help to the categories for which special visas are permissible. More controversially, a further suggestion would be that spending on such child-support could be made tax-deductible by families, as should be spending on daycare centres.

---

[32] Interview with Osawa Machiko, Japan Women's University, Tokyo, 30 November 2017.

7. Legislate for binding quotas for political representation

The idea of using affirmative action, generally in the form of quotas, to achieve greater gender equality (or any other sort of equality) is rightly controversial everywhere in the world, for neither the beneficiaries nor the incumbents feel comfortable with the notion of selection on any ground other than merit. In the case of Japanese political institutions, however, such objections carry much less weight: among Diet members, roughly one-third are reckoned[33] to come from political dynasties suggesting that bloodlines rather than merit already play an important role. Both Prime Minister Abe and his deputy, Aso Taro, come from long-established political families: for Abe his father served as foreign minister and his grandfather (Kishi Nobosuke) as prime minister; for Aso, his grandfather (Yoshida Shigeru) was prime minister twice (1946–7 and 1948–54). Moreover, in a parliamentary system voting tends to be very much on party lines, so that the particular individuals acting as representatives matter somewhat less than in other professions.

As mentioned in Chapter 7, as of March 2019 only 10.2 per cent of members of the Lower House (House of Representatives) were female and 20.6 per cent of the Upper House (House of Councillors). In 2018 a law was passed calling on all political parties to move towards gender equality among candidates but it was non-binding. If the government were to legislate for a binding quota for female candidates, party by party, for the next elections of both houses, perhaps of 40 per cent, then given its strong majority in the Diet it ought to be able to push that through, even though there would no doubt be strong resistance among male members of the Liberal Democratic Party. It might be wise to make the initial proposal a 50 per cent quota so that a retreat to 40 per cent could be presented as a compromise. Then prefectural assemblies could be encouraged to follow suit and similar efforts could be made for other political posts. With the next Lower House elections due at the latest in October 2021, such a quota would have a

---

[33] https://www.eastasiaforum.org/2018/03/13/political-dynasties-dominate-japans-democracy/.

strong demonstrative benefit as well as swiftly providing a larger number of potential female ministers for future governments. To avoid the resulting female influx being considered merely temporary the law would need to be made to apply for a minimum period, which could be ten years.

Private actions

8. Abolish (or phase out) women-only universities

Most of the private actions that can be recommended are for companies to implement. But the first is for universities, and it is listed here as the first private action because it is in fact a hybrid of private and public policy. This is that the country's substantial number of women-only universities should be encouraged to become co-educational or to merge with existing co-ed institutions.

Japan is unusual among advanced countries—though not unique—in having many high-quality universities dedicated to educating only female students: Tsuda University, Japan Women's University, Showa Women's University, Doshisha Women's College for Liberal Arts, to name but a few. Some date back to the late nineteenth or early twentieth centuries. Most are private institutions, although there are two national, publicly funded women-only universities, Ochanomizu and Nara, both of which are prestigious. The future of these institutions is therefore largely a private matter rather than a direct topic of public policy. However, the government should nevertheless pay attention to this issue and use whatever leverage and powers of persuasion it can muster to encourage most of these women's universities to merge with co-educational colleges, whether public or private, or to become co-ed themselves. This sort of process has happened in other countries in the past: almost all Oxford and Cambridge colleges turned co-educational in the 1970s and 1980s (now, all Oxford colleges are co-ed and just three Cambridge colleges remain women-only); in America, the originally all-male Harvard College and its women-only affiliate, Radcliffe College, completed their full merger only in 1999.

Surely, some will say, if some Japanese women want to be educated in single-sex colleges they should have this right? There have
been many outstanding graduates of these colleges, including
women interviewed for this book. Many women's universities do a
good job in equipping their female graduates with the skills and
confidence they need to operate in a male-dominated world of
work and have often adapted their traditional courses in subjects
such as home economics and fashion to make them much more
science-based and commercially useful.

All that is fair and true. Nevertheless, the problem is that the
existence of so many specialized women's only colleges, all over
Japan, serves chiefly to perpetuate the divide between men and
women, especially in the eyes of potential employers. It divides
graduates into categories according to their genders rather than
their abilities. It is a form of gender apartheid that reinforces the
gender gap rather than bridging it. Such gender apartheid stands in
contradiction to the government's aspiration of making Japan a
place in which women can shine.

One benefit of mergers would be that the balance of student
numbers and courses that at the top national universities leans
strongly towards medicine and engineering would become more
even, with some more emphasis on the humanities and social sciences, which the women's universities would bring with them. But
another, bigger, benefit would be that the pace of movement
towards greater gender equality would be accelerated by the influx
of female professors, researchers, and students into the merged university. A final benefit would be a more balanced environment for
the men, too. In their future workplaces, they will need to be able to
work harmoniously and productively in teams and divisions containing large numbers of professional women and men. The more
they get used to it at an earlier age, the better.

9. Make human resources policies family-friendly in a modern way

One thing that was noticeable when research interviews were being
arranged for this book was that the entities most reluctant to grant

interviews proved to be corporate and government human resources departments. Many big companies declined to give me access to senior female executives seemingly because they were afraid that comments those executives might make could sound like criticism of the company or would single out a senior female in a way that both she and her male colleagues might find awkward. The most surprising refusal came from the Bank of Japan, whose head of human resources simply sent an answer that he did not consider it 'appropriate' to speak about this topic at this time. This was strange given that the Bank of Japan's record in employing senior women is not too bad: for example, two successive occupants of the role of General Manager for Europe, a job based in London, have been women and one of them has now become the first female executive board director.[34]

What this reveals is that managers are cautious and afraid of criticism, which may reflect the fact that diversity or the lack of it have now become sensitive issues. Many companies know their HR policies will not look good if they are examined too closely, especially those HR policies that have affected the lives and careers of women who are now in their 40s and 50s. Discrimination has occurred within companies, just as was revealed at Tokyo Medical University.

This is not unique to Japan, however. What is crucial is to learn from experience in other countries and to get change started. The most important aspect of HR policies that needs to change more rapidly is the attitude of big companies to job rotation and intra-company transfers. Companies have got used to treating their employees as being totally loyal and subservient tools, men who can be ordered at very short notice to move to the Osaka or Sapporo office, or even to Jakarta, Beijing, or London. Such staff have been expected to accept such transfers unquestioningly. Their families must either be left behind or else must also move at short notice.

Today such a practice is unusual by world standards. In the 1970s and 1980s, similar stories could be told of American or European multinationals. The basic assumption was that a husband worked

[34] https://edition.cnn.com/2020/05/11/business/bank-of-japan-first-female-executive-hnk-intl/index.html

The Tasks Ahead 181

and his wife did not, so the husband could be moved from job to job or place to place at will. This changed in the 1990s, as more women started to emerge in professional positions and more families came to consist of two professionals. When two professionals form a family, neither of them can be moved easily. Two-thirds[35] of all Japanese households now have both husband and wife earning incomes. So it should now be the norm to consider the whole family when making job postings.

The principle here is that the commitment between an employee and his or her employer should be mutual rather than principally one-way. It should no longer be a matter of signing on to obey whatever orders the company gives. The company's orders—in other words, their job rotation and location decisions—need to take the employee's long-term needs in mind and show a commitment to developing and retaining that employee even as they make choices such as about whether to have a family or how a posting might affect their spouse's career.

10. Employers should abolish distinctions between *ippan shoku* and *sogo shoku* career tracks

That realization of the need for mutual commitment is creeping slowly into the HR departments of big and medium-sized Japanese companies as two things change: as the labour shortage becomes more severe, including of mid-level qualified professionals; and as more of the large generation of university-educated women enter their 30s and 40s and so bring with them different needs and expectations about their careers. A big further step, already made in many companies but still far from universal, should be to abolish the common distinction between career-tracks, between the *sogo shoku* or managerial track and the purely administrative *ippan shoku* track to which women have commonly been confined.

The reason why this would be desirable is that it would abolish a practice under which employees are judged at the time when they

---

[35] *OECD Survey of Japan 2019*, fig. 1.15, p. 91.

join a company, a practice which implies that everything that is important to know about a recruit's abilities and character is already known when they are about 22 years old. Such a judgement is necessarily made on the basis of prejudices about all the choices individuals might or might not make during their working lives over the forthcoming 30–40 years, in particular marriage and child-bearing. This practice introduces a rigidity that may have worked in the past when the population of new young recruits was growing but is unwise and self-harming in an era when the population of new recruits is shrinking and labour at all ages is scarce. In future, amid a labour shortage that is likely to be more or less a permanent feature of corporate life, it will make far more sense for companies to allow and encourage employees to move between functions and 'tracks' according to their life choices, family situations, and above all their emerging abilities and ambitions. From the company's point of view, this would be far more efficient, too.

11. Greater early-stage opportunities and development should be given to female professionals

Osawa-san of the Research Institute for Women and Careers has spent many years studying the choices and attitudes of female university graduates. She[36] is an optimist about the changes she sees in the HR policies of many companies, citing Shiseido, Daiwa Securities, UNIQLO, Seven-Eleven, Calbee, and others as firms that have modernized their ways. An important statistic that she points to, however, concerns the very high proportion of female university graduates who quit their full-time jobs voluntarily. Professor Osawa cites a survey taken in 2011 by the Center for Work-Life Policy showing 74 per cent of respondents quitting their initial post-university jobs, compared with 31 per cent in the United States and 35 per cent in Germany. This is not mainly for the old 1970s reason of getting married and having children. More of the American females who

---

[36] Interview with Osawa Machiko, Japan Women's University, Tokyo, 30 November 2017.

quit do so for reasons of childcare than is the case for Japanese women. Instead, the main reason given by Japanese female quitters is dissatisfaction with their jobs, a feeling of being in a 'dead-end'.

This fits perfectly with the story told by Kawai Eriko in Chapter 9. To remind, Kawai-san's first job, even after having gained an under-graduate degree at Harvard University, was in 1981 at Nomura Research Institute. She was given a uniform to wear and made to serve tea. She was told she would have to leave the company when she got married. Not surprisingly, she decided instead to quit and built a highly successful career in finance in Europe. Women are discriminated against by employers of all types, right from the day they enter the company. The *ippan shoku / sogo shoku* distinction is a key part of that, and the discrimination becomes reflected in big differences in pay, too.

If so, then now that companies face a greater need to recruit and retain professional women alongside their men, they will also need to adjust their practices to deal with this more transactional and less tolerant attitude. Professor Osawa, says: 'Companies need to assign women to responsible jobs at an early stage, in order to give them the motivation and confidence to stay and even return after child-birth.' She says companies need to think in terms of five-year phases of development of their staff, especially given the possibility that women will want to have babies. If they are given leadership experience relatively early, 'then they can have a baby afterwards, and then come back.' She cites the Kirin Company as one that is adopting this idea of relatively early opportunities.

12.   Maternity and paternity leave need to be treated not as mere rights but as aspects of career development. Some element of paternity leave could even be made mandatory.

As we have seen, Japan now has one of the most generous laws on maternity and paternity leave in the world. Female workers who leave their company to give birth can stay away until just before their child's first birthday. Fathers can exploit the same rights.

This has been a big step forward, but so far has not been handled either by government or, most crucially, by companies, in a way that necessarily assists the retention and development of able professional women who wish also to become mothers nor to encourage the sharing of roles back at home.

The difficulty that has arisen is that while a right has been created and enhanced, it has not been adequately matched by obligations either on the part of the employer or the mother. It is not easy, in any organization anywhere in the world, to accommodate the absence of a key member of staff for several months or even a year or more. It creates a cost, in other words, both for the company and for the team. What this requires is some planning on both sides. The employer has to build the expectation of women leaving to have children and then returning into its budgets and its career development strategies. In the modern world, a maternity absence is not an isolated or unusual case: in fact, it needs to become normal. The employee, in turn, has to think hard about how her absence on maternity leave will affect her career path, about what she might want to do on her return, and about how the timing of her return will need to assist not just her but also the company. It needs to be a mutual decision and a shared planning process, in other words.

A female member of the Upper House (House of Councillors) has made a bolder proposal: that taking paternity leave should be made mandatory. Matsukawa Rui did not specify in her article[37] the length of leave that she thinks should be made compulsory—after all, maternity leave is not compulsory—but her argument carries weight. As a way to promote a more even sharing of household chores and childcare, while also forcing companies to make some systematic provision for parental leave, the idea of making it obligatory for a new father to take, say, one month's leave makes a lot of sense in a corporate culture in which without some form of compulsion paternity leave is very unlikely to become standard. When in January 2020 Koizumi Shinjuro, the popular 38-year-old Minister

---

[37] Matsukawa Rui, *Mandatory Paternity Leave Is the Key to Womenomics*, AJISS-Commentary 281, Association of Japanese Institutes of Strategic Studies, 20 December 2019.

of the Environment who is a son of former prime minister Koizumi Junichiro, announced that he planned to take two weeks of paternity leave (while still attending cabinet meetings), it prompted some criticism which implied that to do so represented a dereliction of duty—to the government and not to his family, of course—but was also praised by campaigners for better work-life balance as setting a good, if rather minimal, example.

*   *   *

Japan's future depends on the opportunities that can be given to its people and how well those people prove able to fulfil their potential. People, male or female, represent the country's only natural resource but also a great asset. The productiveness with which that resource is being used has been declining for the past thirty years as insecurity has become widespread: the truth about the so-called 'lost decades' is that the real loss has been of human capital and of the creativity and productiveness at which Japan used to be thought of as the best in the world. And one huge reason for that loss is the unjust and short-sighted way in which women have been treated by employers of all kinds and at all levels, even as gender equality has been making much faster progress in the rest of the world.

Let us finish, then, on a positive, optimistic note. As one of my final interviews for this book I went to Shinjuku to visit the Sompo life insurance company and to talk to the firm's chief executive, Sakurada Kengo.[38] He had been recommended to me as an advanced, pro-diversity corporate leader by an HR specialist who has studied the gender diversity issue from the inside, Achilles Michiko[39] who works for SAP Japan, the software firm. I wasn't disappointed, though Sakurada-san left me with the clear sense that even at his company, there is a huge amount more to do.

Sompo's policy, he said, is not just to talk about diversity but to implement it. Sakurada-san argues that diversity is not just about gender: 'It is about our mentality, our employment practices, our nationalities, our ages.' He sees diversity as a necessity, a requirement

---

[38] Interview with Sakurada Kengo, Sompo Life Insurance, Tokyo, 16 May 2018.
[39] Interview with Achilles Michiko, SAP Japan, Tokyo, 14 February 2018.

of the modern, technological age. 'For Facebook and other technology companies, diversity has been made into a huge source of value and growth. And those technology companies now have a bigger market capitalization than Japan's whole GDP.' He sees insurance as being especially in the line of fire of fin-tech (financial technology) innovation.

As a result, Sompo's policy has become to find good, talented people to recruit from outside the company in mid-career in order to bring in new ideas and new expertise, a practice that in the past was rare among big, established firms who preferred lifetime employment and loyalty. He says the firm has also switched from paying and promoting according to people's input to doing so according to their output: to be result-oriented and mission-oriented. This has been achieved, he says, about 80 per cent at executive level but is taking longer to implement in operations because the employment terms of operational staff are more based on practices among clients. Pensions have been made portable if staff apply for jobs in other subsidiary companies, including those abroad. An order has gone out to the corporate HR departments that among new recruits, one-third should be in mid-career, in order to keep the company innovative.

How far do you expect to go in recruiting and developing women for managerial positions? I asked him. He said that 30 per cent is achievable. 'But right now,' he said, 'only one executive position out of fifty is occupied by a woman. It's a joke.'

The task for every Japanese chief executive like Sakurada-san over the next two decades is going to be to change this. The task for women is to demand that it be changed. The task for government is create the environment in which it can be changed. The joke is coming to an end. It was never funny.

Index

Note: Japanese names are presented in the traditional form with family name first followed by their given name. The abbreviation '*f*' refers to figures in the text.

For the benefit of digital users, indexed terms that span two pages (e.g., 52–53) may, on occasion, appear on only one of those pages.